# THE LOGICS OF MADNESS

# THE LOGICS OF MADNESS
## On Infantile and Delusional Transference

*Salomon Resnik*

Routledge
Taylor & Francis Group

LONDON AND NEW YORK

First published 2016 by Karnac Books Ltd.

Published 2018 by Routledge
2 Park Square, Milton Park, Abingdon, Oxon OX14 4RN
711 Third Avenue, New York, NY 10017, USA

*Routledge is an imprint of the Taylor & Francis Group, an informa business*

British Library Cataloguing in Publication Data

A C.I.P. for this book is available from the British Library

ISBN-13: 9781782203780 (pbk)

Typeset by V Publishing Solutions Pvt Ltd., Chennai, India

# CONTENTS

# FOREWORD

It is a great honour for me and it gives me great pleasure to write the foreword to *The Logics of Madness: On Infantile and Delusional Transference*, this new book by Salomon Resnik.

Each new book by this author is a meaningful event for the psychoanalytic community, not only because of his eminence (Resnik is recognised worldwide as an expert in the field of the analysis of psychosis), but also for the substantial clarity, richness and helpfulness of his extended contribution to our daily practice, thanks to the originality and depth of his vision regarding mental life in general and psychoanalytic relationships more specifically.

I had the good luck to meet Salomon Resnik in Venice, some forty years ago, when I was working there as a young psychiatrist at the local hospital. Together with other psychiatrists and psychologists, I participated in a psychoanalytic group that became a fundamental starting point that led, for many of us, towards further analytical experiences and professional careers; but above all it was an unforgettable, intensely personal experience for all of us.

It was clear from the very beginning that Resnik had achieved a real knowledge about (and familiarity with) the deepest levels of the human mind, and that his technique was in absolute continuity with his perception of the complex transference developments and vicissitudes that characterise the psychoanalytic adventure of each patient.

We quickly realised that he had a special capacity for creating an understandable continuity between the early internal stages of mental functioning and the adult Ego, the interlocutor who worked in the group session with him and with the others; and he was able to depict in a very realistic way the pathological defences, reactions and underlying "logics" that condition the mental organisation of human beings when they find themselves in seriously regressive or fragmented states and in other dramatic conditions.

At the same time, he was able to convey to us a constant feeling of transformability and the capacity for re-establishing a different, more integrated level of organisation: a positive attitude that kept the door open to the possibility of real change and, in the end, to hope.

Furthermore, I remember with genuine admiration his skill in interpreting effectively some very complex and apparently quite meaningless dissociated material: this element is highly specific to the ability to get in touch with the psychotic dimension.

As a matter of curiosity, some dreams evoked at that time in the group mixed typical Venetian scenarios—water, ships, old palaces etc.—with unusual and terrifying natural events, such as earthquakes, tsunamis, storms and so on. The connection between these different dimensions (which would have disconcerted most of us) was mastered in an absolutely reconstructive and re-compositive way by Resnik, at both the individual and group level: an example of what I would define as a good integration of "analysis IN the group" and "analysis OF the group".

To tell the truth, I am constantly surprised by the number and quality of Resnik's observations, reflections and creative suggestions—they are still so much alive today in my memory—and by the way in which they flow so easily from my preconscious when I am at work: they come frequently and spontaneously to my mind as appropriate, helpful tools, in accordance with the variety of occurrences that take place during psychoanalytic sessions, and particularly in highly difficult and delicate clinical situations.

Since their original authorship is absolutely clear in my mind (they bear an obvious Resnik brand-name ...), I consider their appearance to be a sample of sufficiently successful introjective identification with the object: they are partial, related to a specific tool, there is recognition of the source and also sincere gratitude and admiration with respect to Salomon.

Forty years later, and after having followed this great author through many of his papers, books and conferences, I am once again able to experience the shareable depth and brilliance of his psychoanalytic work thanks to this essential, dense, powerful and valuable book.

The author's style is absolutely fascinating: it alternates concepts, clinical reports, autobiographical narratives and memories that integrate with one another, while reconstructing his personal progressive approach to the psychoanalysis of psychosis and the implementation of his scientific knowledge and technique in such a difficult field.

In addition and in the background, Resnik's geographical (I would say: the "psycho-geographical"!) journey from Argentina to Paris, to London, to Venice, through different social, cultural, historical, linguistic and analytical realities, is extraordinary in itself.

His unique capacity to evoke, to quote, to connect with and to integrate the many historical figures he personally met (for example, Melanie Klein, Herbert Rosenfeld, Wilfred Bion, Donald Winnicott, and many others with whom he worked intensively); the institutional scenarios of his activity; the obvious complexity of the patients he successfully treated for many years and the variety of extremely demanding clinical experiences that he has had … all these elements build up the scientific and human patrimony he so generously gives to colleagues old and new with this new book, a real gift.

I thoroughly recommend it to all colleagues, and I want particularly to encourage young psychologists, psychiatrists and psychoanalysts to "stay inside it for a while"—not only to study it (that goes without saying) but also, I would add, to "experience" it in its very nature and substance as a fundamental text leading to a much better understanding of what psychosis and psychotic mindsets are, and of how psychoanalysis can work also in that area, one which is traditionally inaccessible to other human beings.

*Stefano Bolognini*
*President of the International Psychoanalytical Association*

# ACKNOWLEDGEMENTS

I want to thank the colleagues at Karnac Books for all the work they have done concerning this new book.

This time I had the privilege of establishing a personal relationship with Rod Tweedy. I discovered that we have something in common concerning poetry: his interest and work on William Blake. That reminded me of a Christmas present from my friend Hilary in 1960 in London when I was living in Hampstead. The book was a wonderful edition of the complete works of Blake.

I was familiar with the *Marriage of Heaven and Hell* and his paintings but I found the full collection of poems and prose absolutely wonderful.

At the end of *Marriage of Heaven and Hell*, Blake writes: "The Angel who is now become a Devil is my particular friend; we often read the Bible together in its infernal or diabolical sense, which the world shall have if they behave well." He goes on: "I have also The Bible of Hell, which the world shall have whether they will or not" (Blake, 1956, p. 191).

Working with psychotic patients confronts us with the tendency to splitting, idealisation and persecutory or depressive feelings. Heaven and Hell may then become equated somewhere with Freud's opposition and confrontation between Eros and Thanatos.

Rod's advice about adding a subtitle to the book was useful and I have chosen "On Infantile and Delusional Transference".

I have in mind a personal experience in my own psychoanalysis with Dr. Herbert Rosenfeld, which began in 1958. One morning I arrived at the door of his house in Woronzow Road in St. John's Wood and pressed the doorbell several times, but nobody answered. I felt very upset, thinking that Dr. Rosenfeld was perhaps unwell or had forgotten me. Then, after a while, my analyst opened the door as usual. I felt reassured but still upset and a bit angry. We went together to his studio and I lay down on the couch.

I still felt disturbed, like a little child, and I complained: "Why didn't you open the door?"

After a while, Dr. Rosenfeld answered: "You didn't cry enough."

As to the delusional transference, I have in mind an analytical session with "David" in London.

David—a schizophrenic patient whom I liked very much and who was very attached to me—during a particular session he reacted to an observation of mine by saying: "It is exciting."

"What is?" I asked him; I was looking at the same time at one of his eroticised congested ears (it was very red). He said: "What is exciting is to look in your mind and see how your thoughts copulate with each other." At the same time he was moving his mouth like a little baby sucking his mother's breast.

He found it difficult to get up from the couch at the end of the session because of his attachment to that maternal, erotic transference with me.

The next day, he came to his session and said: "When I left the couch yesterday, I was very upset and cross, and the first beautiful girl with nice big breasts whom I met in the street, I stopped her and said: 'Suck your own tits.'" In my mind, I imagined that girl running away.

I wanted also to express my admiration and gratitude to my friend and colleague David Alcorn. I could not at first remember when I met him for the first time, so I asked him. He replied: "Dear Salomon, I have just looked up some old papers of mine—the first time I worked with you was in 1991, twenty-four years ago! This was when you were the guest speaker and clinical mentor for our local group meeting here in Caen, and I was translating some material for you. You presented an introductory lecture at the University, and that was followed on Saturday and Sunday by our clinical meetings. It was in March 1993 that I first worked with you at rue Bonaparte!"

Since then I gather that he has been very interested in my style as an analyst and person. David became also a good friend and discussant with me. He was able to translate some of my French books into English (e.g., *The Delusional Person*) and at the same time he used to help me a lot with my own writings in English as a critical commentator and corrector. He used to like very much to come to my studio in Saint Germain des Près, in Rue Bonaparte and he said once that "that place was for him like the *atelier* of a poet".

I do believe that psychoanalysis is an art and each one should develop his or her own style. I also believe that for the patient the analyst as a person is very important, because independently of any analytical school, what is important is the relationship from person to person.

# ABOUT THE AUTHOR

**Salomon Resnik** is a full member of the Argentine Psychoanalytic Association, specialising in the psychoanalytic treatment of psychosis in both children and adults. After meeting Melanie Klein at an International Congress of Psychoanalysis, he decided to move to Europe, studying first in Paris then moving to London to attend the seminars of Klein and Wilfred Bion. With the support of Winnicott, Klein, Foulkes and Esther Bick, he helped set up a therapeutic community for young people with psychosis at the Cassel Hospital in Richmond. He currently lives and works in France and Italy. His published work in English includes *The Theatre of the Dream*, *The Delusional Person*, *Glacial Times*, and *Mental Space*.

# INTRODUCTION

The idea of the logics of madness was born from my experience as a psychiatrist and psychoanalyst working for almost seventy years in different social contexts. In the Netherne Hospital near Croydon in 1958, I was in charge of a therapeutic community of young psychotic patients. There were seventy patients divided into seven groups with whom I would work in a group therapeutic context two sessions per week. At that time I was attending a seminar on social anthropology by Raymond Firth at the London School of Economics, and I presented to him some of my work. He was very interested, particularly when I told him that one of the seven groups wanted to work on their own, without my being present. He asked me what sort of patients they were. I answered that in most cases they suffered from mystic delusions. After reflecting for a moment, Firth said to me that it was obvious from a *logical* point of view that, if in their delusions they were in contact with mystic figures, they could not accept my presence, since I was simply a human being. That comment was of considerable help to me: in their own delusional world, those patients were at another level of existence, one in which a human being like me, a psychiatrist and psychoanalyst, had no *place*.

However, since delusions are not always stable, in some periods of crisis the patients became more "human" and more accessible, to the extent that sometimes they were able to understand that their logic was a delusional one.

During that year, a young American anthropologist, Anne Parsons, daughter of the famous professor Talcot Parsons, visited us at the hospital. She was carrying out a comparative social anthropological research study on possible differences and similarities in the cultural features of schizophrenia. She sat in as an observer on one of my groups for a few days. She told me that in her research in South Africa and in other countries she had discovered that, unlike neurotic patients, psychotic patients did not present many significant differences as to their overall symptoms. This could be taken to mean that each psychotic patient lives in his or her own world and system of values in which cultural aspects have little impact on delusional beliefs.

I have a patient suffering from schizophrenia whom I have referred to as "The frozen man" (Resnik, 2013) and who told me recently: "You know, in my old philosophy (he meant his delusion) everything was logical, but cold and without feelings. I thought at that time that there was a perfect Aristotelian logic, because it was *pure logic* without the interference of any kind of emotion." In fact he was at that time a petrified and cold being. He has changed since then: he feels alive and comes up against the kind of problems that everyone else has in this very complex and difficult world. The psychoanalytic process acted for him as a sort of humanisation that was able to transform the "frozen" man into a "human" one.

Another patient of mine was obsessed and deluded with his erotic attachment to people wearing thick glasses—people suffering from myopia. I did not understand very much about what was going on until he admitted in the course of a session that he had paid 500 Euros for a pair of thick glasses that a young African in Venice was wearing. That African man was selling glasses, not particularly fine ones, but my patient wanted to buy his own glasses. When I asked him why, he replied, referring to the young African seller: "Because I wanted him to be almost blind like my father who used to wear thick glasses and who loved my sister very much but not me. I wanted him to be blinded by love of me."

In this way, he was able to construct a psychotic syllogism, something along the lines of:

"I want to be loved."

"Love is blind."

"I will be loved by everybody if they are all blind."

Obviously this is an "insane" syllogistic deduction or a delusional misunderstanding based, shall we say, on an Aristotelian way of thinking.

What I want to emphasise is that my way of working with psychotic delusional patients is both a therapeutic approach and a method of research concerning the specificity of the logic of thinking that characterises each patient. I am very interested in the concept of style, not only that of the analyst but also that of a particular patient in terms of a form of identity. This implies a human approach in the psychoanalytic treatment of very disturbed patients who must come to terms with the real identity and ways of being of the psychoanalyst as a person.

In my book *The Delusional Person* (Resnik, 2001), the original version of which was my first book to be published (some forty years ago now), I make it clear that each patient is a person in his or her own way. We should always bear in mind that, for ethical reasons, the intimacy of very disturbed people who have lost at least in part their own identity demands an approach that is highly respectful. In that sense every therapeutic approach is also a kind of reparation—and to a considerable extent a restoration of the self in his or her relationship with a very complex and disturbed world. Bion would perhaps have put it thus: "making the best of a bad job".

I hope that in this book the reader will find an extended clinical psychoanalytic and psychiatric confrontation between "normal" thinking—the kind typical of ordinary daily life—and pathological misunderstandings that have been transformed into strong convictions. The nature or matter of their logical constructions thus becomes very important. Some individuals will have a metallic, petrified, hard or frozen conviction, not easily accessible to normal transference situations. This requires a full clinical investigation into the nature and matter of the so-called "logical conviction".

Sometimes these certainties may be rich, as in the case of the analysis of Schreber's memoirs, which stimulated Freud into writing a paper and offering a personal interpretation of that very exciting delusional book. Indeed, in psychiatry we used to speak of poor and rich delusions.[1]

In my view, Schreber's delusional world, as he describes it himself, is a significant contribution to the concept of psychotic transference before that concept itself came to be developed. When he spoke in terms of Flechsig's[2] rays influencing his own body and mind and producing transformations, he meant unconsciously that he was experiencing a specific kind of disturbed transference situation that nowadays we would describe as delusional. Schreber's delusional experience is an interesting model of a delusional "truth", the bizarre logics of a disturbed, intelligent, and creative mind.

In this book, I describe my various psychoanalytic experiences with very disturbed psychotic patients and my research into their different ways of psychotic thinking. My hope is that the reader will find this exploration not only interesting but also useful.

## Notes

1. See my own point of view on Schreber's memoirs, in Berke (1998).
2. A reference to Professor Paul Flechsig of the Leipzig University Clinic.

# CHAPTER ONE

# The logics of madness

"Madness" is a word that has been around for a very long time, and has been differently expressed as insanity, lunacy, mental derangement, and "melancholy". In his sixteenth-century *Treatise of Melancholie*, Timothy Bright wrote of mental disorders which begin with the presence of melancholic symptoms. In his book, he speaks about "a disposition of the mind altered from reason or else a humour of the body [...] this humour is of two sorts: natural or unnatural [...]". Obviously, Bright was still influenced by Hippocrates' concepts of "humours" (i.e., temperaments) and about the consciousness of sin related to the religious system of values of his time. When he speaks about "humour", he speaks about melancholic darkness ("dark thick bile").

This theme coincides with Griesinger's book on *Mental Pathology* (1882), in which he suggested that any mental disorder begins with a feeling of loss. The loss of some significant family member or other close relationship (or that of part of the body after an operation or some mutilation or other) triggers a depressive state and melancholic phenomena. For Griesinger (1882), all mental pain concerning physical and psychological separation is a "basic depressive state" related to a "normal" or pathological state of grief and mourning.

The term "psychosis" is a relatively recent one; it was used for the first time in psychiatry by Ernst von Feuchtersleben (1806–1848), a German psychiatrist and Dean of the University of Vienna who wrote *Lehrbuch der ärztlichen Seelenkunde*.

Feuchtersleben not only introduced into psychiatry a new standard and a new methodology but also a number of terms such as "psychiatrics"—nowadays, we would say "psychiatry", "psychosis" or "psychopathology", i.e., mental illness as distinguished from neurosis (a functional illness of the nerves).

When first used, the term "psychosis" referred to psychic disturbances different from neurosis and nervous "organic" illnesses such as polyneuritis. This is to some extent the opposite of its modern usage, in which psychosis may have an organic basis while neurosis has a psychological one. German psychiatrists such as Grühle would speak of "endogenous psychosis", perhaps to differentiate this state from reactive psychosis. Later, for Charcot and Freud, "neurotic" meant psychogenic, while "psychotic" was at least in part organic.

In ancient Greek, philologically the term meant a movement of the psyche.[1] Psychosis is somehow related to metempsychosis—a mythical conception used in Babylonian times (and, later, by the Greeks and by Plato in particular): the "psyche" or soul can leave the body (Meta: beyond) in order to "travel" and animate another body—animal, vegetable, astral, etc.,—or to be born again. For the ancient Greeks, the "soma" (body) was close phonetically and conceptually to the word "sema" (grave): our first *habitus* is our body, where we live and die ... To be born means to leave the original mother/*habitus* and come out into the open, into space, in order to inhabit the world.

Hippocrates, with his clinical acumen, described a case of "puerperal insanity" known today as "*post-partum* psychosis".

Gregory Zilboorg's *A History of Medical Psychology* (1941)[2] is an important study of the history of madness in our culture. Foucault's *Histoire de la folie à l'âge classique* (1972) is an excellent complement to that work. Foucault investigated the concept of madness in the Middle Ages and described the somewhat strange therapeutic community where mentally ill people were put into a ship called "stultifera navis"; then they had to find their own way to an appropriate port ...

The problem of mental illness is still a complex one; it is a mirror of our complex and always disturbed society.

## Freud and psychosis

An interest in psychosis was present in Freud's work from his early years as a medical student. In addition to his spontaneous humanistic approach to mental illness and to mental suffering as an integral part of life, he felt moved by human suffering and physical and mental pain.

Some close friends of his who suffered from mental disturbance and drug addiction put him in touch with research into the uses of cocaine as a useful anaesthetic. He himself, as we know, made use of cocaine as a sort of remedy for his own suffering when he became ill with cancer.

Freud's approach to mental pain was very much connected in his mind with physical pain. In November 1882, he began his collaboration with J. Breuer, and through him came to know the interesting case of Fraulein Anna O. Freud felt very moved by the mental distress of Anna O. and with her need to split her personality. At that time, people were fascinated by the problem of double personality in literature, in theatre, and also in the field of psychiatry through the research and writings of the American psychiatrist Morton Prince. Prince (1906) was well-known in America for his research into the case of Sally Beauchamp, who presented similar features to those which Breuer and Freud found in Anna O., in particular a split personality. These cases interested Freud a great deal, and led him to a deeper understanding of the phenomenon of splitting (*Spaltung*) and of the delusional and hallucinatory aspects of mental afflictions.

It was during the treatment of Frau Emmy von N. in 1889 that Freud used the word "unconscious" for the first time (in a footnote to his report of the case). Freud argued that we had to assume the existence of something mental that is unconscious and employed that assumption for the purposes of scientific investigation. He went on to argue that the concept was necessary because the data of consciousness have many gaps in them, both in healthy and in sick people (Freud, 1915e, p. 166). The unconscious is a language, a latent memory and a fundamental psychical process which underlies all others as regards the human organism and life in general (Resnik, 2006). The unconscious follows its own rules and laws, as Freud points out in several of his papers; it is a fundamental part of his metapsychology. There are three papers written by Freud which I find essential for my discussion of the logics of madness—"The antithetical meaning of primal words" (Freud, 1910e), in which he suggests some enlightening ideas concerning the networks of the unconscious, its rules and laws, and linguistic structure. These concepts were later developed by Ignacio Matte Blanco (1975) in his book *The Unconscious as Infinite Sets*.

The second paper which impressed me very much is his study of chronic paranoia, the case-study of Frau P., which appears in his "Further remarks on the neuro-psychoses of defence" (Freud, 1896b). The third paper is the famous paper on Schreber (Freud, 1911c).

## A case of chronic paranoia

The protagonist of Freud's paper, Frau P., gives us a crucial understanding of Freud's personal development concerning his feelings about the transference "psychosis" and the concept of unconscious projection. For a considerable time, he thought that paranoia was also a psychosis of defence, an extremely complicated one to treat since it is based on a delusional conviction. Like hysteria and obsessions, according to Freud, it proceeds from the repression of distressing unbearable memories. In my opinion, this does not go far enough: real paranoia—which is not the case of Frau P.—is an inflexible and petrified ideology, difficult to deal with. Freud argued that paranoia must have a special method or mechanism of repression. One could say that the persecutory feelings of the patient require him or her to build up a powerful mask, a solid wall, a defensive element against a dangerous and threatening world. Freud's paper is fundamental also in that he there defines, for the first time, the term "projection",[3] as we shall see later.

He reports the case of Frau P., a woman of thirty-two years old, married and with a child two years of age. In her mid-twenties she became confused and depressed. A few months after the birth of her child, she showed the first signs of paranoia: she became uncommunicative and distrustful, showed aversion to her husband, brothers, and sisters, and complained about her neighbours. According to her, the neighbours were beginning to be rude and inconsiderate towards her. She thought people had something against her, although she had no clear idea what. Then she added that people in general began to show no respect for her and to do things against her. We know from the classic descriptions of paranoid schizophrenia and from the psychoanalytic approach to psychosis that ideas of reference which lead to delusions of reference, described first by Karl Wernicke then by Bleuler as *Eigenbeziehungen*, usually begin in the "neighbourhood" of the psychotic patient. It would seem that the inner persecutory feelings are thrown into the nearest available surrounding space, then, later, if the degree of persecution increases, the projection becomes more "athletic", to paraphrase a term used by Bion—and so become "cosmic" as it were, going up into other planets. For the moment, let us come back to Frau P. walking in the street ...

She complained that she was being watched by people in the street, who were able read her thoughts and so knew everything about her. One evening she thought that she was being watched while undressing, thereby adding an erotic element to the picture of her unwilling exhibitionism. She was describing a transformation in her world, which from our point of view could be seen as a distortion of the world-picture.

In addition, she experienced strange symptoms in her body. One day, when she was alone with her housemaid, she felt a sensation in her lower abdomen, and thought that the girl had at that moment an improper (i.e., sexual) idea. These erotic sensations increased, and she felt her genitals "as one feels a heavy hand" (Freud, 1896b, p. 176). Then she began to develop horrifying sexual hallucinations of naked women showing the lower part of the body—the pubic region, and pubic hair, sometimes with male genitals. All this delusional somatic distortion added to her distorted transformation of the world. Here we have through Freud's description an excellent picture of the beginning of a delusional universe.

She went to Freud for treatment in the winter of 1895. Freud notes that her intelligence was undiminished in spite of all her delusions and hallucinations. Influenced as he was at that time by Breuer's technique, Freud was aiming at the removal of those hallucinations and treating her persecutory feelings in a case which he diagnosed as paranoia. I consider this paper to be one of the most inspired of Freud's writings concerning the understanding of the delusional world and the mechanism of projection and projective identification, already present here and developed later by Melanie Klein.

The other paper which I consider essential for the understanding of the language of the unconscious is the one that was inspired by K. Abel's book *Uber den Gegensinn der Urworte* (1884); it was in the autumn of 1909 that Freud wrote that seminal paper on the antithetical meaning of primal words. He mentioned Abel again in a footnote that he added in 1911 to *The Interpretation of Dreams* (1900a), in the chapter entitled

"The means of representation in dreams". On page 318, Freud writes, *"the most ancient languages behave exactly like dreams on this point"*.

In that sense, a single word may sometimes carry two quite distinct and, indeed, contradictory meanings. Abel demonstrated that particularity not only from ancient Egyptian sources but also from the Semitic and Indo-Germanic languages.

In his paper on antithetical meanings, Freud writes about the way in which dreams treat the category of contraries and contradictory elements. Dreams, he argues, disregard the meaning of "no"; that notion seems not to exist. Dreams show a particular preference for combining opposites into a single unity or for representing them as one and the same thing.

I shall develop this aspect with reference to Matte Blanco's ideas on the symmetry of the unconscious (Matte Blanco, 1975).

## Dreams and the unconscious

In my book on dreams (Resnik, 1987), I quote Matte Blanco's words on the dream stage: "It is three-dimensional in form, but the content of what is acted out upon it is multidimensional." The dream stage is like a signifier that is constantly being transformed: it may be flat and spread-out, or blown up out of all proportion until it loses shape.

My work on psychosis, psychotic thoughts and dreams has led me to conceive of a multiple complex topology that is "multi-dimensional" (cf. Bion's metatheory (1992, p. 244)) or a-dimensional (Matte Blanco). Dreams and psychosis are the fields in which the concept of multiple dimensions helps our understanding of the unconscious. Matte Blanco quotes Freud (1900a, p. 312): "They are not infrequently trains of thought starting out from more than one centre, though having points of contact. Each train of thought is almost invariably accompanied by its contradictory counterpart, linked with it by antithetical association."

Freud speaks in that chapter about a complex structure in which the component parts are disposed in a manifold logical relationship to one another. They can represent foreground or background (at the same time), chains of evidence, and counter-arguments. We could say that Freud had already the intuition that contradictory perceptions and "logics" can co-exist in the same space and time, if that is conceivable for the Unconscious. I believe that the concept of space and time in the unconscious is a juxtaposition of different times and spaces, apparently in disorder as they would be after an earthquake. In his book *Le Temps Eclaté*, André Green (2000) talks of the proto-history of mental phenomena as being a collection of unconscious splinters, as after some kind of "Big Bang".

Freud's paper on the antithetical (symmetrical) meaning of primal words runs, therefore, parallel to Matte Blanco's notion of the symmetrical quality of the unconscious as a structural reality. According to Matte Blanco, in psychosis, different ideas that have nevertheless something in common can be understood in an asymmetrical fashion so that they may be communicated on a conscious level.

## Symmetrical thoughts and delusions

Melanie Klein's clinical experience greatly contributed to our understanding of a living unconscious with its own rules and its metaphysical implications. Her paper on "The importance of symbol formation in the development of the ego" (Klein, 1930), and Hanna Segal's text on "Notes on symbol formation" (Segal, 1957) play an important role in this paper, particularly when I speak about proto-symbolic equations in symmetrical thinking.

The delusional world, inspired partly by the logics of the unconscious, appears as a kind of philosophy of life. Often, it is a very disturbed and disturbing conception of the world, which has its roots in the impact of a traumatic experience upon a fragile or rigid unconscious world. The capacity to reach some plasticity of the mind has to with the basic fragility of being. The rigid or inflexible obsessional and paranoid personality can collapse during some pathological or unavoidable therapeutic crisis. Some analysts would argue that there can be no true analysis without critical situations or crises (in Bion's words, "catastrophic change").

Melanie Klein's case study of "Dick" suggests the concept of symmetrical (or "symbolic equations"). I shall develop this point later.

## The logic behind delusional thinking

Psychotic patients are preoccupied with deep metaphysical issues. As they cannot deal with everyday reality, they have to construct their own universe. This universe follows some of the principles of the unconscious in opposition to some conscious principles concerning communication with others and the reality principle.

A patient of mine who suffered from schizophrenia believed that *he* was the creator of a new *"Big Bang"*, and therefore that the universe (his universe) would be in danger if his tendency to expansion continued and turned into an explosive event. This patient, whom I shall call "Edmund", was a young man of twenty-two years old. Although he saw himself as quite a small person, sometimes a "little sad mouse", he felt that if he became a "big man", a sort of new god, he would endanger the *"living gods"*. For him, the living gods were his father and grandfather, both important god-like figures in the French judiciary. If the little mouse became inflated and turned into a big creature, a giant with cosmological power, they would be in danger. The idea of envy and unconscious, omnipotent envious attacks on the idealised figures was very much present in his delusion and transference situation.

In their presence, he felt small (this was true also of the transference situation) as though he, the personification of the Big Bang phenomenon, could never be more than a *"little bang"*: a little mouse. By becoming a "big bang", in his delusional state, he would have tremendous universal power. He once made a drawing of his brain: it looked like an inflated/inflatable armchair—a throne; as a king/god, sitting on it, he would be the motive force behind the intelligence of the universe and achieve perfect happiness. From this deified brain, a new rhythm would preside over the universe. This rhythm, with its element of time, meant that he could be also a sort of new Chronos.

He believed that, by constructing this picture of himself and of the world, he would be able to rid the universe of all suffering. In his expansion, he believed that he would be infinitely powerful. One of his frustrations was that he could not enter into the minds of other people—as if he were blind to otherness. I recall that the French psychiatrist, Jules Séglas, used to describe the feeling of *"cécité mentale"*—mental blindness—which, of course, is not the same thing as physical blindness. But Edmund was not always powerful; sometimes he became deflated or exploded. He would then find himself in a state of mental and physical depression—or in one of expansive excitation. When his delusional omnipotent world went into a crisis he would then become deeply depressed. Voices would say that he was a failure and not the centre of the universe at all, as he would have liked to believe. He then felt that he was a failure and wanted to die. Like Christ, he would be crucified in the centre of the globe of the Earth to pay for his delusional arrogance.

The "Big Bang" idea, which he himself called "a scientific delusion", upset him very much, because it could demolish the existing world of which he also was part—and so everything he liked in the world would be demolished too. Some feelings of guilt and "responsibility" appeared from time to time.

He remembered that in his initial crisis, after feeling shy and small, he took some hashish and began to have delusions in which he thought he was going to give birth to a new universe. To eliminate the old universe—and to attack the power of his father and grandfather figures (also of the great father, i.e., God and the analyst in the analytical field)—would provoke a human and cosmological punishment.

The delusion of grandeur in his big-bang fantasy meant also that, if he had a breakdown in which he might explode, all the fragments of his body and mind would turn into stars and planets in his own universe. In such a case, everything would revolve around him—but he would be alone in that universe, journeying endlessly through outer space.

To come down from his delusional world, to "come down to earth" meant that there was a price to pay. That price was to experience a state of crisis, a "break-down"—in other words, to come down in bits and pieces. Expansion of his ego (delusional ego) did not preclude a dispersing projective identification within the almost-limitless boundaries of an expanding universe; indeed, in his geographical and historical delusion, the one went hand in hand with the other.

After a few sessions, Edmund felt that there was a kind of time-bomb ticking away inside his stomach, which was equated with the sound of the "Big Bang". I understood—and I was trying to work this through with him—that his body was not prepared to hold on to such an enormously delusional project. On the other hand, he used to "collect" (over many years) experiences of frustration and loss which were so painful that he could not digest them. At one moment, a major part of his delusional fantasies was somatised in such a way that he became unable to mentalise and keep hold of such a painful burden; he could not come to his sessions and, because of the unbearable pain in his stomach (he felt that he was going to explode), he consulted the medical team ... in the *Hotel-Dieu* hospital, in Paris—literally, in the "House of God"!

Expansion and inflation of the self became, in Edmund's case, an uncontrolled delusional aim. To contain in his own body such tensions and pain demanded that, from time to time, he needed a subsidiary body—a hospital (God's one)—to help him contain his "visceral complaints". In a dream during his analysis *he saw his gut falling out from the sink*—it was uncontained by the sink. This meant that, in opening up his delusional world and his body-and-mind, he would experience a kind of "evisceration". Beyond his excessively powerful energetic state, when he became deflated, he felt that he was almost dead: a corpse, rather than a living body. In the dream, everything took place in the toilet-part of himself (i.e., it was related to evacuation and to cleanliness). But, at another moment, when he became deeply depressed, the taps on the sink meant that he was trying to control—to shut down—his unbearable need to weep and the intolerable fear of losing his innards.

Between the alive and dead parts of his body ego, between narcissism and destructive power, to become God starting a new universe was an omnipotent and unbearable illusion. In a case like that, disillusion becomes an intolerable narcissistic wound, and an unbearably painful depression: a feeling of loss.

Later, Edmund complained, via members of his family, that he no longer wanted to come to his sessions because he felt too depressed. This was a normal expression, I told him, of his delusional deflation and narcissistic depression (Resnik, 2004, 2011). I call narcissistic depression a state in which the ego-ideal is wounded—it is not simply a matter of loss of the delusional object, but also of an enormous hole in the self.

Later, I discovered that the somatic crisis in his stomach (which prevented him from coming to his sessions) began on the underground when he overheard a woman talking to another person about God and religion. I returned the question to him: "Why indeed, if you yourself, during a Big-Bang crisis, are the creator of the Universe? How can a monotheistic, 'monolithic' god believe in the existence of another one?"

"It all started when I wanted to be free," he replied. "I was young— a young adolescent—and very afraid of the dark. One day, I had a terrible nightmare. When I woke up, the nightmare continued. My bed folded up like a trap on me" (he made a movement with his hands that resembled a mouth swallowing). "At that point," he said, "a horse began to gallop all over my body." I then remembered that the word *"nightmare"* gives the image, in the night, of a mare that is out of control and galloping crazily. His freedom was a mad freedom. Borges (1985), in his lecture on nightmares, mentions Victor Hugo's *"cheval noir de la nuit"* (the dark horse of the night).

R. D. Laing (1960) used to say: *"Madness need not be all breakdown. It may also be breakthrough. It is potential liberation and renewal as well as enslavement and existential death."* In Edmund's case, psychotic freedom was an attempt to break free of the cage—but it only put him into another one (the globe of the universe which he drew in his crucifixion delusion resembled a spherical cage). To be deflated from his delusional and cosmic universe implied an unbearable and painful depression that neither his mind nor his body was able to contain. This is the basic dilemma between the psychotic and the non-psychotic parts[4] of the personality (Bion, 1957), one that involves awareness or denial of internal and external reality. The psychotic or broken self splits up into many scattered fragments and particles that are projected or expanded in an uncontrollable way—like a crazy horse out of control, in other words a real *night-mare*. On the other hand, awareness and bringing back the fragments may imply an unbearably depressive and maddening feeling; it is here that the danger of committing suicide arises.

The attack against another god, when the child part is treated by the internal mother like a "little god" (a sacred piece of a narcissistic mother's body), becomes a struggle without end.

One day, Edmund came to his session and told me that he was very impressed when he saw somebody in a passing bus smiling at him. In French, smile is *"sourire"*—and from that head-in-the-bus-window came a voice that said "Big Bang" repeatedly in a mocking but sad way. I invited Edmund to associate, since at that period he was hallucinating mocking voices which did not take his "scientific" delusion seriously. After a pause, he said: "I have a picture in my mind of a little mouse [*"souris"*, in French] which is unhappy; it's in a small room, perhaps a toilet, where there is also a sink." I asked him about the sink. "There are taps, they're closed. It's for containing my tears." I interpreted to him that after a crisis in which all his delusional apparatus blew up from a "big bang", he again became a deflated "little bang", just like a little unhappy mouse that feels like crying.

Edmund, the "Big-Bang" boy, reminds me of Edgar, a twenty-three-year-old man who suffered from a mystical delusion. While walking in the street, at night, he saw a black car, with all of its doors closed. He interpreted this as meaning that that car was of some importance to him. He thought to himself that God, through this black car, was saying to him that he was the person chosen to tell everyone in the vicinity that the end of the world was coming. In the course of the therapy, I asked

Edgar what kind of car it was. He raised his right hand slowly and solemnly, and said: "Fiat". I added: "Fiat lux—therefore 'let it be done'; you were the black angel announcing the end of the world."

I find that in many schizophrenic patients the "Big-Bang" theory plays a very important role. The acute psychotic crisis is experienced as a cataclysmic phenomenon in which the tensions between symmetrical feelings and thoughts are near to consciousness (asymmetrical thoughts following Ignacio Matte Blanco) and their mental space cannot hold contradictions. This inner war between delusional inflation and deflation, between symmetrical and asymmetrical thinking is a painful one.

As Delsemme (1994, p. 366) puts it: "Our era has an open mind about the cosmic origins of the adventure of being human." The scientific fantasy or awareness of the Big Bang stimulates unconscious fantasies about the origins of our planet and of our life. In many people, and in particular in psychotics, the interest in metaphysical and cosmological preoccupations is fundamental.

As the delusional world expands, the capacity for containment of mental space becomes critical and tends to break out or to break through. When this happens, massive and violent projections of a reality felt as "inner emptiness", according to the patient, appear brutally. In the fullness of that emptiness, the inhabitants of the patient's inner space become persecutory objects and are expelled far away in the cosmos and therefore in time. The multiple dissemination of ego parts and inner objects tends to expand, as if they needed to take possession and control of the whole universe. A patient of mine in a therapeutic group, whom I shall call "Otis" once said: "I cannot think, there is an emptiness, a big hole, a dark hole, between my nose and my skull; then it becomes a sort of sponge, a terrifying one which sucks everything around and inside. This sponge is always in expansion. It is a disturbing and uncomfortable experience in which all the galaxies, in all the surrounding universes are being taken in, sucked in like into a black hole. It reminds me of a time when I used to take lysergic acid at the beginning of my illness". This was a sort of avid sucking emptiness …

Another patient, "Ellis", who was a member of the same therapeutic group of schizophrenics, said: "I have in my head a shapeless magma that tends to expand and eat up everything. Inside the magma there is a mixture of broken words or parts of phrases." Both Otis and Ellis were trying to establish a dialogue between an unbearable sponge and a dreadful magma …

The concept of emptiness does not imply nothingness, but rather the presence of a mass and of particles equated with nuclear forces, parts of a psychic and physical electro-magnetic field.

Delsemme uses terms such as "Big-Bang" and inflation; he writes of nuclear forces, where *quarks* (elementary particles) exist, and of a breakdown in the symmetry of forces that provokes a change of state. This often means a change in the properties of symmetry: for instance, ice creates crystals, the symmetry of which is different from that of water. On the other hand, when ice melts, it absorbs a certain quantity of heat: the latent heat of the change of state. Latent heat comes from a change in entropy, a concept that Freud found useful. The temperature of the water is often lower than zero degrees Celsius without turning immediately into ice—this is the phenomenon known as *supercooling*.

These phenomena take me back to my book *Glacial Times* (Resnik, 2005) and also to my recent book *An Archaeology of the Mind* (Resnik, 2011). Scientific hypotheses and findings are often related to delusional ideas in many of my patients. This is because they are concerned with "real" metaphysical issues and with cosmic dimensions. In a way, psychotic patients may be dealing, in their flight from daily life and terrestrial problems, with universal "scientific" intuitions. Glaciation is an anaesthetised state in which the properties of a body, object of nature or human, change; heat and pleasure that cannot be coped with become a particular ideology. A delusion is a specific system of ideas that lie outside those commonly held; they have their own logic, laws, and rules.

Freezing, which is a way of avoiding mental feelings and unbearable persecutory states, may suddenly thaw during a crisis in which the delusion becomes related to the end of the world and of the universe.

In psychotics, "scientific" fantasies and hypotheses appear within a breaking world in which the ego needs to conceive of an "explanation" either of the ending of the universe or of the birth of a new one. Between these two states, there is perhaps a phase of transition. What is the quantity of energy that becomes free to suggest a new expansion or inflation? According to Delsemme (op. cit.), there is one theory of inflation that offers an explanation of the Big Bang in terms of a quantum fluctuation of an original emptiness.

My thinking on these issues also involves the concept that Melanie Klein (1930) called "symbolic equation". During a session with her patient, "Dick", an autistic boy with almost no language, suddenly said the word "dark" as he stood between the double doors of the therapy room; Klein interpreted this as "Dick is inside dark mummy". The boy became afraid and asked when his nanny was coming to fetch him. In another session, he said "cut", and Klein gave him a pair of scissors. He tried to scratch the little pieces of black wood which represented coal, but he could not hold the scissors. She cut the pieces of wood out of the cart, gave them to Dick, and he threw the damaged cart and its contents into his drawer, saying "gone". Klein said he was cutting faeces out of his mother. He ran to the space between the doors and scratched them a little with his nails—he was identifying that space with the damaged cart and the mother's body, which he was attacking. A persecutory climate appeared, because at the beginning of the next analytic hour, he cried when his nanny left him. I would add that the nanny coming to fetch the little boy, and therefore implying the end of the session, was also a traumatic "cutting-off" experience as regards his link with Melanie Klein, just as an important dialogue was being set up between them.

One day, when Dick saw some pencil shavings in Klein's lap, he said "poor Mrs Klein". Then he went to the window and said "poor curtain". This would mean, I think, that Dick was establishing a relationship between what was going on at the window and Klein's skirt. I would say that there was a symmetrical phenomenon between the "skirt of the window" (the sun? the moon?) and the material of Melanie Klein's containing lap, which held the pieces of the broken bits of wood of the pencil that had been "attacked"—and also of course of the bits and pieces of the little boy himself, cut up by the teeth of a devouring world (the projection of his cannibalistic greed).

Klein says that there were rudiments of symbol formation in this sequence (Klein, 1930, p. 227). My impression is that Hanna Segal, in her paper on symbol formation, tried to develop these aspects of Klein's session with Dick. However, I would take issue with Segal's description of what occurred here: I do not believe this to be a "symbolic equation", because a symbol is never "equated" with the symbolised object—it is a transformation. These phenomena are rather what I would call "*proto-symbolic* equations".

Melanie Klein mentions the term symbolic equation which applies, according to her, to "things, activities, and interests which become the subject of libidinal phantasies" (op. cit., p. 220). She suggests also that the child who desires to destroy the organs (penis, vagina, breast) which stand for the object establishes an equation between organs and objects of anxiety. In some notes that Mrs Klein added to that paper, she shows that the early forms of symbol formation are precisely symbolic equations (p. 428).

I would suggest that these early forms are not really symbolic yet, but related to a kind of symmetry and therefore have to do with proto-symbolic thinking.

For Matte Blanco (1975, p. 69), symmetrical modes of being are part of the *Ucs* (unconscious) system. He says that the noun "the unconscious" is not just a quality but a mode of being. "The quality of being unconscious was a necessary consequence both of its structure and of the structure of that other mode of being described by Freud as the 'conscious' or 'consciousness'".

In another part of his book, Matte Blanco writes of the interaction between symmetrical and asymmetrical relations (op. cit., p. 283). This concerns the relationship between unconscious and conscious modes of being.

In Edmund's delusional world, there is a phonetic proto-symbolic equation between *"sourire"* [smile] and *"souris"* [mouse]. In Dick's case this would be a *"textural"* proto-symbolic equation between the curtain and the material out of which Mrs Klein's skirt was made. In Hanna Segal's paper, when the violinist moved the bow with his hand, this meant for him a symmetrical repetitive movement as in masturbation; I would call this a *"cinetic"* or *"kinetic"* proto-symbolic equation.

While I was in London, I attended Bion's seminars and had personal supervision with him over three years; I remember that he was particularly preoccupied by the idea of scientific thinking in psycho-analysis. He used to say: "What can we do in order to express scientifically feelings and thoughts which have neither colour, nor form, nor scent nor smell?" My answer, given my interest in phenomenology and the "visibility" of the unconscious, would perhaps be that feelings and thoughts have the colour, the form, and the smell of our own body. The great neurologist and psychiatrist, Pavlov, suggested that the mucous membrane of the bowels turns red whenever a blush comes to the face—and in fact that this reddening of the mucous membrane precedes that of the face. We know that in psychosomatic medicine, guilt and shame can be manifested in many ways such as bodily feelings and bodily thoughts.

The other schizophrenic patient whom I mentioned above, Otis, dreamt about a monkey (in French *"singe"*), that was moving its head.

Otis said that the dream reminded him of nothing in particular, except for the fact that he was at that point working and he wanted to learn about sewing and dress-designing. He could then associate to the trademark "*Singer*"—the sewing-machine that his mother worked on at home when he was a boy. In this example of phonetic proto-symbolic and kinetic (the moving head of the monkey, the shuttle on the machine) equations, Otis was expressing his wish to bring things together in his mind, with some kind of coherent pattern (or design) in his imagination; hopefully a pattern that would not be delusional.

Sewing ("*coudre*"), like knitting ("*tricoter*") has to do with the word "*pensum*"—which was a weight of wool distributed to maids for spinning (Partridge, 1958, p. 481) in Roman times. This, then, was a "task". At that time, spinners and weavers would be paid according to the amount of wool or thread they used. "Knitting" becomes a model for thinking, for putting things together, with a good "*Singer*" psychical apparatus. In another session, the patient drew a distinction between true imitative thinking—in French, "*singer*" means to imitate, to caricature, and has the same root as "*singe*", i.e., monkey—and being himself, with his own "thread" of thoughts.

In *The General Laws of the Bipolarity Symmetrical-Asymmetrical or Unconscious-Conscious*, Matte Blanco (1975, p. 311) discusses the symmetrical and asymmetrical aspects of the mental apparatus as equated with unconscious and conscious systems of the mind. I find his concept of the unconscious as infinite sets very enlightening. I have chosen to discuss symmetry because it is particularly suited to my exploration of proto-symbolic equations. In my way of conceiving the inner world, I do not have the impression that there is a "gap" between conscious and unconscious—it is more a matter of the continuity of different qualities of the mind that are part of a state of one-ness. This enables me to argue that in dream-interpretation what is called "latent" is already "present" in some way in the manifest aspect. In the intuitive experience of the transference—as in the art of the interpretation of dreams and delusions—what comes "before" in time is co-present in living space, and therefore may be read as such.

It is precisely the "logics of symmetry" within the unconscious that has to do with the principles of psychotic thinking and delusions. Dreams and delusional thinking have something in common, though they are not identical phenomena (Resnik, 1987).

The different clinical examples in the present paper give a graphic illustration of some of my points of view as regards psychosis, which is my main field. In a paper on non-verbal communication, Matte Blanco (1968) speaks of sensory and extrasensory communication, a topic that I find very interesting; my own clinical observations (Resnik, 2001) are strongly supportive of this outlook.

I believe also that there are many ways of transmitting feelings from one being to another, which we do not yet fully understand. Sometimes we call it "paranormal" or "intuitive" communication: from unconscious to unconscious. In the chapter of my book (Resnik, 2001) entitled "Language and communication", I give examples of transference phenomena relating to non-verbal and intuitive communication in which psychotic patients are able, as it were, "to read my mind" and vice-versa. For instance, when I took the decision to leave for London, I wrote in English a letter to Melanie Klein (in 1956), saying that I had decided to have further analysis there with Herbert Rosenfeld and to follow her seminars. At that point, one of my psychotic patients, who was of foreign extraction, dreamt that she was a little child playing with her analyst with toys and talking in English (her parents used to speak English). Later, in another session the same patient, symmetrically, was lying on the couch, then stood up and put the handkerchief used as a head-rest over my mouth like a gag.

She said "Don't speak a word, don't open your mouth." I was just then thinking about saying to her that I was going to be unable to see her for a few days: I needed a throat operation on polyps (my father died from cancer of the larynx). The patient had obviously "perceived" my fear and anxiety—perhaps also she wanted to safeguard me from her own very violent oral projections. Perhaps such an experience might be called symmetrical; it involves the "climate" of the transference situation at a particular moment.

There is also a sort of geometry of silence in which, travelling in a straight line or sometimes involving the subject with some sort of circular waves, some particular feelings have a strong impact and effect on the other person. That may be distressing, but it is also enlightening. It has to do with psychotic anxiety and perhaps with discovery.

In the paper by Matte Blanco which I have just mentioned, he speaks also of the logical structure implicit or explicit in the unconscious aspects of the mind of the patient and of the psychoanalyst during the transference situation. Matte Blanco says that in daily life, a kiss can be conventional, without any real affection; at other moments, it can be cathected with concern and real emotion.

To come back to the logics of the unconscious, Matte Blanco gives the example of Professor Bumke in Germany. A psychotic patient was bitten by a dog, and went quickly to ask for help at the local hospital—but to the dental surgeon's department! The symmetry in that case was between the biting teeth and the tooth marks that needed care by the specialist doctor who would heal the victim of those biting teeth. Some symmetry of that kind is at work in Otis's example between the monkey and the sewing machine Singer—something that would "sew" together the parts of his split mind.

I recently came across an example of bi-logical thinking in my own work. I needed to change the appointment with Otis, Ellis and other members of that therapeutic group because at the time of the session, I was invited to participate in a live radio programme, broadcast on the "France Culture" channel, about schizophrenia. I told them I would see them the day before. I thought it was better to tell them, for ethical reasons, in case they listened to the programme. Otis, who is usually very punctual, did not come to the session. We decided to phone him during the session, to ask him what happened and he told me:

"But our session is tomorrow at 7.30 p.m."

"Don't you remember that's the time I'll be "live" on France Culture?"

"Yes," he answered. "I know that you'll be speaking on the radio at that time. But I was expecting the group session to take place anyway."

At that moment, Ellis said: "For an atom that could be the case." Ellis, an expert in nuclear physics, was apparently not only concerned with qualitative aspects but also with quantitative atomic phenomena (he was doing research into identifying and "counting" atoms). He had not spoken for several years and was unable to work properly; it was only a short time before that he became able to express himself and work in his laboratory. When he started to talk, he said that he had been living for a long time in a tower.

"Samuel", another member of the group, also schizophrenic—his delusional experience was taking place in another time, in the Middle Ages (he claimed to be a soldier of Carolus Magnus)—asked Ellis: "To which era belongs your tower?" Ellis answered: "It's in the Middle Ages." From Middle Ages to Middle Ages, both patients managed to find the time to meet together in space … Time in psychosis, as in dreams, is very peculiar. A minute can replace centuries and vice-versa: psychotic history lives in different times and spaces. The double transference, from the patient to the analyst and vice-versa, needs to find the right instant of Utopian space-time.

Later, Ellis said: "The tower is empty, and nobody is there." "Who is 'nobody'?" I asked. "Perhaps a hidden or invisible Ulysses-Ellis?" I added, following the answer that Ulysses gave to Polyphème in *The Iliad*.

I think this kind of Beckett-like dialogue is a good example of symmetric bi-logical thinking, in which the principle of contradiction does not exist: different forms of logic can run in parallel to one another.

I have found also that, in psychotic thinking, the principle of reality and unreality must be taken into account (delusional reality is "true" for the patient), as in the former example; in addition, sensory data and delusional voices may have different meanings.

Symmetrical phenomena as proto-symbolic equations and other qualities can be "equated" meaningfully for the psychotic mind. The best definition of what is a hallucination was given to me by Samuel, who said: "Once upon a time, my hallucinations were real thoughts." "But unbearable ones, perhaps," I suggested to him, ready for evacuation as Bion would have argued.

I feel that inner persecution and unbearable feelings of loss in fragile psychotic personalities can be calmed down only by multiple, evacuative, projective identifications that aim at dispersal. Those projections into living objects encircling reality transform the landscape of the universe into a disorganised one—or, perhaps, reorganised in a delusional sense.

In his *What is Life?*, Erwin Schrödinger (1944, p. 73) writes about reorganising disorganised molecules or objects through bringing back aspects of a disorganised world. In his way of expressing these matters, an organism maintains itself stationary at a fairly high level of orderliness (i.e., at a fairly low level of entropy) through "sucking" orderliness from its environment. Otis in another session spoke of a terrible white cloud that "sucked" all his thoughts and feelings and made him empty. "It is a nasty cloud which is enveloping my mind and that of others too—and sometimes the whole universe."

To my mind, however, thanks to a psychoanalytic and semiological investigation of the transference, the healthy parts of the personality— or the healthy fragmented aspects mixed up with insane or psychotic fragments projected into the landscape of formal reality—can be rescued and reintrojected. The patient, of course, must be ready to take "disintegrated objects" (the psychotic and non-psychotic aspects) back into his mental space and to allow them to become genuine thoughts again. For me, thoughts are "living thoughts", emotional ones—ones that are no longer petrified or frozen.

The idea of entropy was very important for Freud, and in a note to "Recapitulations and problems", the final chapter of "From the history of an infantile neurosis" (1918b [1914]), he wrote: "Entropy is the force which, according to the Second Law of Thermodynamics, tends to make certain physical changes irreversible [...]" (op. cit., p. 116). My own clinical experience with psychotic patients over almost seventy years has, however, taught me that the changes brought about by schizophrenia can be reversed. I would say that in psychotic patients a chaotic inner world spreads out projectively and expansively into the whole universe. What we call re-introjection in psychoanalysis is a way of helping inner emptiness to be inhabited again, by the use of therapeutic transformations: to change unbearable, persecutory and highly depressive objects or experiences into bearable ones.

To the physicist, life seems to be orderly and lawful behaviour of matter, but to psychoanalysts the unconscious is also living bodily matter, which has its own rules and follows its own laws. Mental illness results not only from lack of ego cohesiveness but also from intense persecutory and depressive anxiety that the individual finds unbearable.

The delusional world is a pathological solution which consists in making use of the power of the unconscious to construct, via deluded hallucinated thoughts together with verbal and non-verbal communication, a "new world", a new illusion. At that point, disillusion is narcissistically too distressing, so that the self is unable to negotiate with the reality principle.

This chapter forms part of my most recent research into the unconscious and the delusional way of thinking—in other words, its logics—in psychotic patients. Madness is never completely mad. Psychoanalysis is an exploration and a form of treatment for people who are suffering and cannot make any sense of thoughts and feelings that seem to be nonsensical. It is also a matter of instants in time—there are moments when the person who appears to be mad gives some sense to what is going on and makes it meaningful. In Bion's supervision of my two schizophrenic patients, he said to me: "Your psychotic patient, in this session, is not psychotic; he is at this very moment neurotic."

Verbal and "non-verbal" communication play a very important role in the understanding of proto-symbolic phenomena and symmetrical thinking. Matte Blanco's contribution to the language and logics of the unconscious, and the implications of Freud's paper on the antithetical meanings of primal words, are always present in my mind as I work with schizophrenic patients: their systems of logic are "familiar" with the language of the unconscious.

In the analytical situation, there is one very important element: the climate or *Stimmung* that is prevalent. Some forms of silence may be a tearful, crying and obscure but meaningful expression of the mind. Sometimes silence becomes a necessary thoughtful pause to be respected. There is also from time to time a shadowy link … until the other living shadows of the mind come back into a new opening of the transference situation.

## Notes

1. *Psukhe* has the sense of "mind"; its derivative *psukhoun* means "to breathe life into, to animate", whence psychosis.
2. Gregory Zilboorg was born in Kiev, and worked in Saint Petersburg as secretary of the Minister of Labour for the provisional government of Kerenski. Later, he moved to the United States, and his teaching at Columbia University is looked upon as highly important.
3. Strachey notes that the first appearance of the concept of projection, and indeed of the term itself, in Freud's writings appears in a letter to Fliess (Freud, 1950a [1887–1902], Draft H).
4. While I make use of the term "parts" of the self, following the traditional Kleinian manner, I have always in the back of my mind that Dr. Georges Daumézon, as a psychiatric semiologist, was unhappy with this kind of compartmentalisation. From a phenomenological point of view, I too would rather speak of "aspects"—which I think of as more global conception of a complex reality which can be seen differently according to the moments and specific outlook or vertex, to use Bion's term.

# CHAPTER TWO

# Delusional space and time*

This chapter is based on my research into the phenomenology of space and time in schizophrenia, at the time when I worked in the Cassel Hospital, Richmond, England. It was in 1959 that I was given the opportunity of working as a senior medical officer in a hospital for neurotic and borderline patients. The colleagues who introduced me to this hospital were Donald W. Winnicott and Malcolm Pines, my consultant, who put me in touch with the medical director, Thomas Main; all of these practitioners knew of my work with autistic children and, in particular, with adult schizophrenic patients, and they allowed me to undertake the treatment of some borderline psychotic inmates.

I came to the Cassel after working in a therapeutic community in a major mental hospital in Surrey. At that time, in 1958, I had the opportunity of studying the meaning of "mental" and physical behaviour in space and time of borderline and psychotic patients living within the same community. At the Cassel, I worked mainly on an individual basis

---

*This chapter is an extended version of a paper published in Ahumada, J. L., Olagaray, J., Richards A. K., Richards, A. D. (eds.) (1997). *The Perverse Transference & Other Matters. Essays in Honor of R. Horacio Etchegoyen*. Northvale, NJ & London: Aronson.

with the patients, within the wider therapeutic community, and was able therefore to focus my attention both on individual sessions and on the general body language of the patient within the community.[1]

As I write now about that experience, I shall include my present knowledge and clinical expertise in order to illustrate certain aspects of psychotic phenomena in the transference situation and in daily life. I am attempting to understand, together with the patient, what "logics" patients make use of in their delusional world. I believe, following Herbert Rosenfeld and Bion (the former was my analyst and the latter my supervisor), that complete madness does not exist as such. Some part of the personality is always preserved, and the analytical process can enable us to get in touch with it and to work through the psychotic aspects. I believe also that whatever occurs in everyday life during psychoanalytic treatment has to be looked upon—this is one of the aims of this book—not necessarily from a delusional point of view or as an acting-out but as an "acting/talking" in which patients are able to express bodily feelings and behaviours as a mode of existing and being in the world.

From a multi-dimensional point of view of the delusional mind, as I have tried to show in the preceding chapter, the psychotic—like the dreamer—is simultaneously present at different points in space and different moments in time, although he or she is quite unaware of the fact. Therefore, as in a dream, psychotics are able to play several roles in unrelated places at the same time, and thus avoid the limits and constraints imposed by the ordinary three-dimensional world.

The notion of multiple dimensions in space came to me when I read Freud's book on dreams (Freud, 1900a), where he writes that the dreamer is present simultaneously in each of the characters of his dream. Ignace Matte Blanco (1975) went on to develop that idea. Taking this as a starting-point, we can think of the "psychotic state of being" from a multi-dimensional out-look/in-look. Like Bion and Matte-Blanco, I believe that psychotics are constantly attempting to escape from the limitations imposed by the formal three-dimensional world and to express their own system of logics and beliefs. The dilemma is that, although they may escape from a finite, confined world, they cannot cope with infinite timeless space. As Samuel Beckett put it so eloquently:

> Emptiness, silence, heat, whiteness, wait, the light goes down,
> all grows dark together, ground, wall, vault, bodies, sat twenty

seconds, all the greys, the light goes out, all vanished. At the same
time, the temperature goes down, to reach its minimum, say freezing point, at the same instant that the black is reached, which may
seem strange. (1995, p. 183)

To be oneself—to accept one's own mental and bodily space—is often
extremely upsetting for the psychotic patient. This is a theme I develop
in my chapter on "Personalization and Cotard's syndrome" in my
book *The Delusional Person* (Resnik, 2001). Such patients cannot tolerate the experience of being themselves in their own body, and often
they become phobic with respect to their own feelings and thoughts,
which they then try to evacuate through pathological projective identification. This situation was described by Melanie Klein in her paper
"On identification" (1955), based on Julien Green's extraordinary novel
*If I Were You*.

Freud (1923b) speaks of bodily ego and psychic ego as two aspects of
the same being, and emphasises the fact that the ego should not remain
an imaginary entity but ought to exist mainly as a bodily ego. As Freud
says (1923b, p. 26): "The ego is first and foremost a bodily ego; it is not
merely a surface entity, but is itself the projection of a surface."

Psychotic patients need to have an experience of their own body but
at the same time they feel this to be intolerable. The psychotic ego is
both very fragile and over-sensitive. In order not to experience unavoidable feelings and to prevent mental suffering, psychotic patients
tend to attack their own mental apparatus during their acute psychotic
breakdown, precisely because it puts them in touch with an unbearably
painful world (Bion, 1967). The paradoxical result is that they develop
hatred for their own mind.

In re-reading this paper I cannot avoid adding few words about a
schizophrenic patient whom I have at present in analysis—from time
to time, he feels very dispersed in space and time. It is as though parts
of his body scheme were broken-up and scattered throughout different
places and times. He often says that he felt accused by his mother for
having "destroyed" his mother's perineum when he was born. He experienced his mother's complaint as a maddening experience in which he
became confused with his mother's body and felt that his own body
was often split up into bits and pieces; sometimes he is no more than a
mind-head. This appears in one of his dreams, in which at times he was
a deprived and therefore destructive dog's head, without a body; he felt

that he wanted to bite his mother's head off (it too was separated out from her own body). His catastrophic delusional interpretation of his birth was experienced as an attack on the mother by the disruptive baby coming out into the world and destroying both his mother's body and his own. Very recently, he had another dream—a very short one, simply a number: "Five five zero". After a silence, I asked him what associations came to him. He said: "One five with another five." As he was saying that, I looked at his hands—they were folded in such a way as to give the impression of a hole between the fingers. I commented that it was as though five fingers were trying to hold the other five fingers in such a way as to produce a hole (the zero in the dream), which could contain his dispersion and his tendency to escape from being wholly one person.

In sub-acute and chronic conditions, the attempt to escape from their own mental space involves the search for another space, another place and another time in which to live. This aspiration is based unconsciously on the fantasy of choosing another body or another planet in/on which to be, to live. In mythical terminology, this unconscious fantasy went under the name of metempsychosis—a transmigration of the *psyche*, characterised by the basic psychotic belief of being reborn into another body or into another nature. It could be a tree or a star in heaven ... The body in this mystic belief is left behind in an endeavour to be re-born elsewhere (i.e., into another *nature*[2]). The main purpose of this is to escape from one's own original body, or "house of being", in other words to get away from one's own destiny. Sometimes, such patients try to be everywhere all of the time—the equivalent of being nowhere. They may sometimes become invisible or a phantom or just a shadow ... My experience with the personal logics of any delusional world has taught me that psychotic "athletic" projective identification (see also Bion) never leads to real identity. Nobody can become oneself into another body or self, or bodily self. Recently, an introverted adult patient who is quite autistic said to me: "When I was a child, I was always behind my mother. I used to tell her everything and she used to listen to me. But, later on, I myself became simply the shadow of my mother." Some patients (and, indeed, psychotherapists) believe that the therapeutic process has simply to do with telling the analyst his or her problems, without making use of free associations. If that is not interpreted in terms of an attempt at escaping from oneself and getting inside the other person as a container, one that will do their thinking for them and keep control of their scattering, no improvement will ever take place. That was the case of my patient before she came to me; indeed, during her analysis, she would complain and demand that I be like her mother and contain her feeling of dispersion and lack of a real self. In such cases, patients always find it difficult to be a real person. They feel cast out of time and space, they do not have a real body.

According to Winnicott (1945), this is a disturbance of the process of personalisation and of becoming aware of one's own body. If individuals are to be themselves, to experience their own personal mental space and to exist *in time*, they will have to accept the space and time that life has bestowed on them and to recognise that their body belongs to them as part of being a person-as-such. Psychotic patients run away from any hint of sensations and feelings that might imply being-oneself. They avoid living time (Bergson's *temps vécu*) and living within their own space in an attempt at escaping from being themselves, which would imply being able to tolerate mental suffering. The price to pay for this kind of existence is non-living—the impossibility of being wholly alive. The self turns into a mechanical contraption along the lines of an automat or a computer. In the psychotic crisis, one of the first lines of defence against mental pain and catastrophic experience (Goldstein, 1951) is to freeze and immobilise the ongoing flow of time.

Freud (1933a [1932], p. 59), writing of the fragility and vulnerability of the psychotic self, compares the psychotic ego to a crystal. "If we throw a crystal to the floor, it breaks; but not into haphazard pieces. It comes apart along its lines of cleavage into fragments whose boundaries […] were predetermined by the crystal's structure." Freud went on to develop his ideas (in his 1937 paper on "Constructions in analysis") related to reconstruction and restoration. "The analyst […] works under more favourable conditions than the archaeologist" (1937d, p. 259). In the transference, patient and analyst can make contact with lost and scattered fragments of a broken and petrified living time. The archaeological artefacts which fascinated Freud were, for example, those of Pompeii or the tomb of Tutankhamen. "All of the essentials are preserved", he writes, "even things that seem completely forgotten are present somehow and somewhere, and have merely been buried and made inaccessible to the subject" (op.cit., p. 260). How are we to bring all these fragments to light?

Following in Freud's footsteps, and borrowing ideas from Melanie Klein, Herbert Rosenfeld, Hanna Segal, and Wilfred Bion on minute splitting and pathological projective identification, I would like to add my own developments on the archaeology of the transference and the concept of field-work applied to psychoanalysis (Baranger, 1969).

In the acute phase of the breakdown, i.e., during the catastrophic experience itself, the self is broken up into atom-like fragments difficult to detect. Occasionally, some of these tiny fragments impinge on the surrounding landscape and merge with it. I am speaking here of *fragments of reality* (a concept developed later in this chapter) which endeavour to remain in concealment while playing a kind of hide-and-seek with the analytical/archaeological task. These fragments are very often *camouflaged*, the aim being to avoid a persecutory and threatening world. For example, an *"arborescent fantasy"* spreading out into the landscape may attempt to get *inside a leaf or a tree trunk* in order to conceal its nature. The surrounding countryside then acquires a magical quality. Perhaps it will have to wait until a *storm* breaks before it reveals its true essence and be identified for what it really is by the observing ego of the patient and by that of the analyst. When persecutory feelings are brought into the transference field, they are weakened, and the ability to deal with mental pain therefore becomes more effective. It is then that the archaeological uncovering of hidden fragments of reality can be undertaken, and the process of reconstructive re-introjection can take place. Melanie Klein's term is reparation, but to stay with my archaeological metaphor of the psychoanalyst as field worker, we could add the idea of restoration.

The issue at stake is not merely one of space and time; just as important is the global atmosphere, the *Stimmung*, the climate, where cold and warm, humid and dry will provide a vibrant and sensitive appreciation of regression as it occurs in present time. In this sense, our work as analysts is a sort of *archaeology of the present*.

In order to provide a framework for my investigation into these hypotheses in the context of the psychoses, I would like to describe a particular clinical situation which I hope will prove useful. Alice M. was a young woman of twenty-five years old, good-looking though somewhat untidy in appearance; she gave the impression that she was confused in space and in time. Following a suicide attempt with medication, she was referred to the Cassel Hospital in 1962, where, as I have mentioned, I then worked as a senior psychiatrist under the guidance of Malcolm Pines as consultant.

Alice M. came from a religious background—her father was a clergyman, and one of her sisters was a missionary. Alice was the youngest of the family. Some months before her suicide attempt, she had begun to have dizzy spells and to feel confused. For instance, when she intended to go somewhere, she would forget her destination (which is also her "destiny"), and become muddled and lost. The same was true of time: when she was supposed to be somewhere at a particular moment (for some prior arrangement or other), she could never remember the time of the appointment, and would turn up at quite the wrong moment.

I began working with psychotic patients in Argentina in the late 1940s under the supervision of Dr. Enrique Pichon-Rivière. He would tell me that I must not expect a psychotic patient to subscribe to the formal space and chronological time of the psychoanalytical setting when the therapy was just beginning. And, as it turned out, Alice M. found it very difficult to share with me our official psychoanalytical time— sometimes she would come late for her session, sometimes too early. This has to do with the difficulty that psychotic patients have in tolerating a defined—and confined—space and time.

At the present moment, I have in France a patient who suffers from schizophrenia. Whenever he becomes confused in his mind and loses all idea of where he is "located", he will ask me questions such as "What is the definition of normality? What is the definition of God? What does it mean to be a *shaman*? Is it the same as being an analyst?" I take all this to mean that instead of looking for a direct answer to his questions as such, he needs me not only to be a subsidiary ego and superego but also to *define*—to bring definitions, to give meaningful boundaries to his time-less and space-less world of confusion. There is always some truth and some logic in our patients' own way of thinking. It is part of our task to get in contact with that logic, with that way of thinking, and with that system of ideas or delusions.

Again, Alice might be physically present with me in the session, but this did not necessarily mean in any *real* sense that she was actually there "with" me in time and in space. This of course made the timing of interpretations extremely hazardous—I first had to "know" whether she was "there" or not, to *define* her in a certain sense.

Occasionally she would look in a particular direction—out of the window, for example—and this I later understood to mean that she was moving away from the *hic et nunc* of the transference situation (from present time) into some far-off point in space.

Alice M. was able to communicate with me—"from time to time"—with a certain degree of warmth and feeling, but quite often she was unable to concentrate. She gave me the impression of being "distracted"—scattered simultaneously over several *loci*. She told me once in a cold, dry, monotonous tone of voice that she held several jobs: "I am a musician, and I play the organ in church on Sundays. I work also as a physical education instructor in another place, and I teach children somewhere else again." In her multiplicity, she became for me a kind of one-woman band. Alice was able to give a picture of her normal and abnormal way of thinking and of her own painful reality. To get in touch with her inner and outer reality meant also to invite her to re-waken old memories and traces of her disturbed mind.

She found it difficult to think—to bring ideas together—and to remember things, and as a result she felt unable to concentrate. She complained once that she was afraid of being "lost" in her own mind, as though she might fall endlessly down into some vast, empty, bottomless mental space—she was suffering from a kind of *internal agoraphobia*. Her inner mental space was experienced as a boundless open space. Occasionally she would suddenly feel "blocked"—paralysed, inflexible, and petrified. At other moments, she lived in a dream world: "Instead of thinking, I dream", was her way of putting it. This was a very apposite remark, because psychotic patients are indeed not only unable to differentiate between wakefulness and sleep, but often are quite unable to wake up. This is why there are some misunderstandings about the ability or inability of psychotic patients to dream. Often, indeed, they are dreaming all the time—but with their eyes open, and they do not know that they are dreaming precisely because they are unable to wake up. This would be true for all of us: if we were unable to wake up, we could not know when we were dreaming and when we were not.

Alice said that she had nightmares during which she could hear *noises* or *voices* shouting at her. This is what I call a "phonetic equation", a particular form of Hanna Segal's concept of symbolic equation. When Alice walked along the street, she felt that people were looking at her and could know what was going on in her mind.[3] From what she said, it was obvious that her experience of life was strange and unreal.

Let me now try to describe a fragment of my first meeting with her. Sitting in the armchair, she seemed far away and frightened, tense and anxious. I did not come too close—I kept some distance (space) between us—because I felt that she needed to get to know me gradually, and also because she might feel herself becoming confused with me, and me with her, if we were in too great a proximity (Rosenfeld, 1950a).

I asked her a question, but she did not answer. She was looking at me in a lively, exploratory way, but when I asked her to tell me something about her personal life, she began to make shaking movements with her head—as though she were shaking something off. I had the impression that this movement was an attempt to get rid of my question (experienced as persecutory) through her ear—to expel her introjections (i.e., what she felt to be my projections). I was trying to approach her cautiously, and pointed out that whenever I said something in an attempt to get to know her, she made this movement with her head. "Perhaps," I said, "you cannot stand my voice. Maybe you feel it is strange and threatening and trying to get inside you." Alice replied: "It's not a voice, it's a noise." "My voice turned into a noise so quickly?" I asked. Alice smiled, and said: "Well, sometimes it becomes a voice again." Here, "voice" and "noise", although still in phonetic similarity, have become more differentiated in meaning and in value.

There followed a long pause, a pregnant silence. She said: "I'm afraid." "Why?" I asked. "The voice is saying that I'm crazy," she replied. Then she began to answer the voice, changing her own voice and whispering, "Keep still, keep still." Sometime later she relaxed and told me that the voice had disappeared. Then she added: "You know, Doctor, the voice that says I'm crazy breaks up into so many little voices. It's driving me mad. The world around me seems so strange and hostile." My feeling was that she did not know which was worse—one big voice calling her crazy, or the fact that if she attacked this distressing voice it would break up into such a troublesome and uncontrollable multitude of voices. How could she be in control of so many points in space from which so many threatening voices were coming? Why did they choose her? What was so important about her?

In another paper of mine (Resnik, 1989) based on Melanie Klein's concept of massive projection, I develop the idea of "dismemberment" not only of the internal object but also of the various aspects of the ego which are in relationship with the internal object. This includes those parts of the mental apparatus concerned with hearing, looking, speaking, etc., together with awareness of reality (both normal and delusional reality) and parts of the ego and the superego. The part that is exploding or being violently expelled consists of a complex, micro-fragmented "material" (bodily) reality. There results from this what we might call a "somato-psychic mutilation". In my view, what was unbearable and painful for Alice was related to the normal and thoughtful aspects of her personality. What was normal in her made her suffer when she was faced with what was not normal. She therefore very often had to deal with both a pathological and a normal way of thinking about the same reality.

In another session, Alice suddenly began to tremble when she heard "real" noises coming from the radio in a neighbouring apartment. Then she was startled when she heard the ticking of a "real" clock. I made a small noise to clear my throat, and she again became frightened and began to move her head, as though trying to get rid of all these noises surrounding and invading her. After a while, she began to panic: the sounds from the radio and the clock were getting inside her. "In the same way," I commented, "as the noise in my throat announced that I was about to say something, and thereby intrude upon you with my words." She listened carefully to what I was saying, but felt that she had to shut herself down and wrap herself up in a tense silence. I remained silent too; I felt there was no point in interpreting what was taking place, because she was experiencing the world around her as turning into one great hostile noise, no matter what I might be able to say. After a while, I felt that the unbroken silence between us was itself becoming too "noisy".

Throughout this phase of her treatment all the formal aspects of the analytical setting—the objects in the room, the chair, the desk, the couch, the clock, my way of talking—had a particularly disturbing effect on her. From time to time, however, I had the impression that my presence in the room was becoming less threatening, less strange, and that she could as a result be less tense.

Alice could not think (make contact with the thoughts in her own mind) or even listen without feeling endangered, because many different situations were felt to create a menacing and invasive atmosphere and even sometimes became equated with concrete, hostile objects or actions against her. In her 1957 paper, based partly on Melanie Klein's earlier work on symbol formation (Klein, 1930), Hanna Segal uses the term "symbolic equation", a concept which does much to further our understanding of this phenomenon. As I mentioned earlier, I would perhaps prefer to speak in terms of proto-symbolic equations,[4] because the patient is not fully able to generate symbols. I would describe Alice M.

as suffering from noise-related phonemic proto-symbolic equations. For her, space was a dangerous place, an unbearable field where distressing messages might get inside her and attack her. Her only recourse was to get rid of (evacuate) all these disturbing introjections, in a true acting-out of intolerable inner and outer experience.

After a recurring period of depression and elation, during which Alice gradually became aware of her fear about other people doing things to her, she was able to recognise what she herself was doing to things and people around her. I believe—and I discussed this with Bion in individual supervision with him—that in the transference (psychotic and non-psychotic), there is a level which cannot be understood simply in terms of acting-out or acting-in; such phenomena should rather be seen in terms of "zones of influence" between two protagonists—we feel that the patient is doing things to us and we are felt to be doing things to him or her. I am convinced that the actual physical (bodily) presence of patient and analyst in the session is not without significance; we are influenced by and are influencing the other by the very fact of our mutual "concrete" co-presence. In this particular atmosphere, the "good" or "bad" products of a "concrete" transference must become part of this dual interplay between transference and counter-transference.

Our means of perception and discrimination—our mental apparatus, as Freud put it—is a very fragile and sensitive instrument, a necessarily delicate one, a musical instrument which in discord as in harmony requires the presence of a skilful tuner. A tuner who has a good "ear", able to perceive the major and minor dissonances and resonances of our living presence, is necessary for making contact with very disturbed patients and helping them to get in touch with their own disharmony. Psychoanalysis is a very creative experience, but often a disturbing one too; the analyst, especially if he or she treats psychotic patients, has to be in close touch with the workings of his or her own mental apparatus, and must appreciate how delicate an instrument it is for working with life.

## Discussion

From patient to psychoanalyst, from mind to mind in the transference situation, what is the meaning of an attuned or synchronic relationship?

What is the meaning of a dys-chronic, a-chronic, or tuneless transference situation? How can an experience of space or of time become disruptive, alienated or alienating?

How does a delusion arise? What does "delusional space" signify? One of the characteristic features of an incipient psychotic breakdown (particularly a schizophrenic crisis) is the transformation of ordinary time and space into something quite out of the ordinary. Normally, relationships are grounded in an allo- or hetero-centric conception of space; the *extra*-ordinary change brought about by such a breakdown is the delusional construction of an ego-centric conception of space and time. Everything that happens at a given moment and in specific circumstances is experienced as being directly connected with the (self-centred) individual; there is no room for a diversity of viewpoints.

This symptom was studied by Bleuler under the name "delusions of reference" (*Beziehungswahn* ), and Sérieux and Capgras (1909) showed how these can develop into delusions of influence and interpretation. I have discussed these topics in some detail in an earlier book (Resnik, 1986).

A young patient of mine, Henry, had a Kafkaesque nightmare during his schizophrenic breakdown. He was at school, when suddenly his body changed into an enormous spider. Little by little, the spider used its expanding legs to take possession of the entire school-space. Everyone in school was immobilised and under his control. In this case, the ego-spider of the psychotic self, like some monstrous amoeba with its pseudopodia, was able to dominate the surrounding persecuting world.

The idea of the ego as an amorphous primitive life-form goes back to a primary regressive state which, I suggest, is pre-objectal—or at least precedes any capacity for projective identification. Etchegoyen (1991, p. 572) comments on a paper of mine (Resnik, 1973) in which I argued that we should not confuse projective identification with *expansion of the ego*. Projective identification implies recognition of a differentiated internal and external space, whereas narcissistic expansion ignores the frontiers of the body and merely extends further and further outwards—just like the amoeba with its pseudopodia, as I have pointed out. Partial extension/expansion of the ego—global expansion was called by Séglas the "delusion of enormity"—involves a primitive viscous ego whose pseudopodia reach out towards the object without recognising the existence of differentiated body limits. For Etchegoyen, this concept is similar to the classic idea of primary narcissism. Melanie Klein makes no hypothesis about the birth of space, yet without space "in between"—without distance—neither projective identification nor object relations are possible.

Paul Federn (1953) often made use of the term "ego boundary". He also uses words like "circumference of a territory" and "ego periphery". This last term expresses the fact that the ego is actually felt to extend as far as the feeling of ego unity can encompass. Federn is here discussing "ego feelings" and their vicissitudes (p. 222). As Freud put it (1923b, p. 26): "The ego is first and foremost a bodily ego; it is not merely a surface entity, but is itself the projection of a surface." He added in a note in 1927 "[the ego] may thus be regarded as a mental projection of the surface of the body, besides […] representing the superficies of the mental apparatus."

In the metaphor of the amoeba, the periphery of the psychic ego is not necessarily a "circumference", but rather an irregular, dynamic boundary, a living one in its most primitive sense. For a human being, this corresponds to the idea of a dynamic body schemata (Schilder, 1950) reacting to "transference relationships" in life. From a phenomenological outlook, the implication is that the human expressive shape is above all mobile. According to Edoardo Weiss's introduction to Federn's book, the concept of ego boundary has to do with the contact and sense of reality and its disturbances, such as the feeling of estrangement with respect to external objects and a loss of reality, as well as the phenomena of hallucination and delusion. Federn's concept of the ego as a dynamic entity and the ego boundary as its peripheral sense organ is implicit, in my view, in Freud's *The Ego and the Id* (1923b).

What is still required, however, is the articulation between the concepts of ego boundary, body ego, and body language. In my first book, *Personne et Psychose* [*The Delusional Person*], (Resnik, 1973 [2001]) I wrote of body language as verbal and pre-verbal (and sometimes non-verbal) expressions of a living body trying to reach—or to avoid—other-ness; sometimes the aim is to induce sympathy or antipathy, or even indifference. I went on to develop a psychoanalytic semantics of the body in the transference situation, depending on the different moments of the experience of "being-with".

What is typical of Alice M., however, is less expansion than minute splitting and projective identification: the multiple fragments of all the figures and objects of the transference space become part of a delusional world. In some cases, fragments of a delusional ego become alienated and alter the meaning of external and internal reality. In other cases, it is as though these fragments induce reality itself to become delusional. In other words, these are "deluding fragments" (which generate delusions) rather than delusional fragments.

I am convinced that it will prove useful eventually to discuss Strachey's notion of "therapeutic alliance" in the light of "agonist" and "antagonist" identifications in the transference space between patient and analyst, as well as within the mental space of the patient and his or her ideology (a delusion is a system of ideas) and of the analyst's personal and scientific ideology in the normal and abnormal counter-transference. This was one of the topics in which both Herbert Rosenfeld and Horacio Etchegoyen (1991) showed interest.

## Notes

1. In my book *The Delusional Person* (Resnik, 2001), I develop my views concerning the body language of psychotic—and more specifically schizophrenic—patients.
2. The myth corresponds on the cultural level to an ancient Babylonian belief and to an oriental Indian tradition; it was later introduced into Greek thinking by Pythagoras.
3. *Beziehungswahn*, or delusion of reference (pathological self-reference), is characteristic of the onset of a schizophrenic condition, and was described and studied by Eugen Bleuler in his book on *Dementia Praecox* (Bleuler, 1911; English translation, 1950).
4. I find somewhat disturbing the misunderstandings that surround the idea of symbolic equation. Melanie Klein introduced the concept in 1930 in her paper "The importance of symbol-formation in the development of the ego". Hanna Segal wrote an important paper on this theme, "Notes on symbol formation" (1957). The misunderstanding is related to the fact that a symbol, by definition, is different from what it symbolises. There is a whole work of transposition and transformation, the elements of which cannot be equated as such. For this reason I prefer to speak about proto-symbolic phenomena which relate to the symmetry and equivalence between two experiences or concepts and therefore represent an archaic level of symbol formation.

# CHAPTER THREE

# Transference in psychosis and the mind of the psychoanalyst

In the course of my psychoanalytical work with psychotic patients, some problems arose concerning the language—verbal and non-verbal communication—used both by the patient and by myself. Free associations are not limited to words and gestures; they concern also the tone of voice, pauses, and the nature or semantics of silence. And also, I would add, the significance of the overall ambience, the atmosphere of the encounter as it is experienced by patient and analyst. This atmosphere is a language in itself, a true ecology of the encounter (friendly and warm, or unfriendly and cold, etc.) in the same way as there exists an ecology in/of the mind (i.e., the atmosphere is such that one can or cannot think). All this is part of a complex cycle of facts and experiences, which can be conceived of as a "living" transference situation.

Following Freud's concept of transference, we could say that the patient is expressing, transferring, transmitting, and dramatising unconscious aspects of his or her personal world, to which the analyst will react equally unconsciously in his or her counter-transference.

I believe that the spontaneity and intuitive style of the psychoanalyst is essential for the patient. Patients pay close attention to the degree of authenticity of the analyst's feelings, especially if they are afraid of expressing their own feelings and thoughts. The more the patient is disturbed, the more pronounced is his or her sensitivity and the need to know what is going on in the mind of the psychoanalyst. On the other hand, one of the main concerns of the analyst is to be aware of what is going on not only in the mind of the patient but also in his or her own mind.

I will try to develop some of these views by narrating and transmitting some extracts from the clinical material of a psychotic patient in the initial stages of her psychotherapy.

## A clinical case

One day I received a phone call from a worried mother, who requested an appointment for her daughter, Renata. She had heard that I had been able to help Basilio, a very disturbed boy of the same age who presented similar symptoms and who used to live in their neighbourhood. She had contacted me in the hope that I might be of some help for her daughter. Although my agenda was already quite busy at the time, we arranged an appointment for the following week.

Renata came, accompanied by her mother and her older sister. Her father was busy and could not join them. Renata is the youngest of the family, a good-looking girl of twenty-five years old. She gave me the impression of being very withdrawn as she moved mechanically. From time to time, she seemed to be a kind of doll—neither a girl nor a boy, but something in between. She looked like a medieval page from some kind of fairy-tale or legend. The mother and her two daughters sat in separate chairs. The mother, who was not only worried but in fact very depressed, started to explain in a sad tone of voice that her daughter had been very introverted and withdrawn since childhood. At the age of eighteen, she had become even more emotionally blocked and shy. During daytime she always remained alone at home, hidden in her room; sometimes she would go out in the evening with a boyfriend.

After the mother and sister spoke, they felt that perhaps Renata would prefer to see me alone. Renata agreed. Sitting opposite me, she remained unyielding and silent. She seemed to be quite indifferent to me and to her surroundings—it was as though she was in a state of being physically and mentally immobile and paralysed. She remained silent and immersed in her own private world; I felt that talking to her would be taken as an intrusion into that world. When I asked her how she was feeling, it was as though I had woken her up. After a moment she answered in a mechanical and monotonous tone of voice:

"I don't feel alive; I am dead."

I asked her when she had died. She didn't answer at once, but after a long pause she replied:

"I am very lonely and I feel isolated. I spend most of the time in my bed or alone in my room." Then, after another pause, she added: "I am not interested in things. Actually, I prefer to be alone." I could feel that she was locked up within herself, so I asked her:

"Do you ever go out?"

"Sometimes, with my boyfriend."

"Where do you go?"

"I go to discos, but I never dance."

"What do you do?"

"I listen to music, it relaxes me and fills me up when I feel empty."

I asked her what type of treatment she had been having. She replied in her usual sad tone of voice that she had seen several psychiatrists and had also been to see a psychotherapist, but only once. She then added that until now she felt that the doctors did not understand her and that her latest psychiatrist (who had made a diagnosis of schizophrenia) had just treated her with drugs which were not very helpful.

She repeated that she was always alone and withdrawn from people, and she became alive only at night when she went to discos with her boyfriend.

"My boyfriend doesn't always seem to be a real person. He sometimes seems to turn into a silhouette or a shadow."

She then appeared to fall back into her dream world, far away, like a lonely, lost star in a dark universe.

I must confess that during this first meeting I tried not to get too close to her; I felt the need to remain distant. However, Renata was also keeping herself away from me. Both of us needed to keep our distance. I found her cold or inhuman at times, like a doll or a statue, but at others more alive, when some warmth would spring forth from her eyes. I was touched by her loneliness and moved by some aspects of her unusual personality.

When the session was finished, her mother and sister came to collect her. We arranged a new appointment before they left. I should emphasise that she always needed someone to accompany her because of her agoraphobia.

A few days before the second session, Renata's mother phoned to tell me that her father wanted to join us. On the day of the second appointment, Renata had decided not to come; her parents, however, did come. The father explained that Renata was against coming this time and resisted any sort of suggestion or supplication.

In my experience, when someone from a patient's family, in this case the father or mother, still keeps an appointment without the presence of the patient, this often means that unconsciously the patient is indirectly communicating through this mediator something that he or she cannot express directly. Psychotic patients are frightened of entering into a close and direct relationship. They need a spokesperson or vehicle to communicate for them in order to avoid the "danger" of falling into a state of confusion and loss of identity. The representative becomes their eyes and ears; in this case, her parents were Renata's instruments for detecting whether I was trustworthy and a "good hospital" for her recovery. Psychotic patients tend to project themselves into the analyst (projective identification) in order to test him or her or to be protected inside the analyst's mental space and/or body ego. They need to avoid the unbearable feeling of being outside in the world (agoraphobia in the transference) or too shut-up and lonely inside themselves (feelings of claustrophobia). Both extremes are intolerable. Renata probably wanted to know through her parents—in particular her father, who seemed to be more active than her depressed mother—if I was the right person to take care of her and to tolerate and understand her. I was therefore the good containing mother capable also of assuming paternal functions (this does not imply that the father or mother did not also have their own personal reasons for meeting me).

According to her parents, it was quite exceptional for Renata to come to the first meeting. "She needed time," was the father's opinion. The father, very tense and upset, was worried about his daughter and wanted me to help him deal with the difficulties of his paternal responsibility at home. He liked to be able to be in charge of situations and to manage the family successfully. The mother, a frightened and insecure woman, was not able to make decisions by herself. She therefore expected her husband to decide for her.

Finally Renata decided to see me again. It was her father who phoned me, on her behalf, to ask for an appointment. I understood that Renata was "indirectly" expressing through her father that she wanted to see me.

When she arrived, I opened the door and as expected her parents had accompanied her. They left her alone with me and told her they would come back later to pick her up. I asked Renata to wait a moment or two in the consulting-room.

When I went in, she was standing. She looked at me, scratching her left shoulder with insistence. I said to her:

"You don't look dead today."

"Why?" she asked, in a detached tone of voice.

"Because I have never seen a corpse scratching itself."

She smiled weakly and said:

"My shoulder is itchy and I feel uneasy."

"Are you cold?" I asked her, remembering her coldness during the first session and keeping in mind that at the end of our last session, I had felt that she was able to transmit to me some warmth. I became, then, the formal container of her warm feelings. Psychotic patients tend to be cold because they cannot contain warm feelings, which are perhaps too painful to experience. If they cannot keep their own warmth, they need a subsidiary body to act as a preserving, containing "storage heater".

She responded to my question about being cold:

"Perhaps less cold, but still cold." Then she added, "You know, I am still dead."

"But what about the scratching?" I asked her

She answered:

"Perhaps I am trying to awaken a corpse in me."

"Through scratching?"

She sat down opposite me. She relaxed for a moment but then immediately became stiff and tense. She gave me the impression of being meditative, but from time to time she would sit looking into the distance, expressionless. She remained for some time in this immobile state. I thought that she was once again immersed in her dream world. After a long silence I noticed, looking at one of her fingers, that she was wearing a bandage. I asked her about it, while realising once again that I was going to wake her up from her personal dream world. She replied:

"I am absent-minded … Oh yes, the cut on my finger," looking at her bandage. "Yesterday I went to the kitchen to cut myself some bread but instead I cut my finger." She looked at her finger and then let her hand fall. She paused and said:

"I am still isolated."

"Cut off from life?" I suggested.

"Yes I am cut off, I am cut off from everything," she said in a lonely sad voice.

I said to her that her illness could mean that she needed to be cut off from the rest of this world and probably from her own. While talking to her I felt that she was looking beyond to another space, another world. She wanted to run away from this present world from her own body and her own mental space. But where to go? Psychotic patients are experienced travellers of the mind.[1] They have a need to escape from their own feelings mainly when they are in pain and feel persecuted. Sometimes I feel that they run away from any kind of feeling—even pleasure, if it becomes just too much for a fragile self. When the internal objects feel in danger, especially during an acute psychotic breakdown,[2] they run away from the body ego, like panicking sailors escaping a sinking ship (Karl Jaspers' metaphor). Even though our discussion was in another language, I could not avoid translating (in my mind) this experience into English and equating a sinking ship with a "thinking ship" (i.e., the thoughts were sinking).

I could feel she was in an ambiguous state: it was unclear whether she was sleeping, daydreaming or awake, so I asked her about this. She replied: "I don't usually dream." After a pause she added: "Oh wait, I have just remembered some fragments of a dream."

"Can we look together at some of these fragments?"

"Yes," she said, "but they are just moments when I am struggling and arguing with somebody."

"But to argue means that you are alive!" Then I added, "What sort of arguments?"

"Well, I quarrel with my father, and at other times with my older sister, I've always had problems with both of them."

After a pause she said:

"Some of the dreams have dogs in them."

"Do they quarrel with you, or you with them?"

"Not at all," she replied, "I like them." As she said this, she looked at me and touched her nose in a rather affectionate manner (the patient's reaction made me aware that my mind had anticipated aggressive feelings, which were not necessarily present, related to the word "dogs").

"They have a good sense of smell, don't they?" I added, taking into account her non-verbal communication.

"Certainly," she said touching her nose again.

I was "touched" by her words and playful gestures and said to her:

"Do you think that we two could relate to each other like friendly dogs?"

I felt as though at this point that some "ludic" (from the Latin *ludere*—to play) or playful aspect of her infantile self was wakening up, which is an important sign of transference development.

Herbert Rosenfeld says that when infantile transference comes to the fore in psychotic and delusional patients, it becomes easier to work with the psychotic part of the personality. Infantile transference requires an analyst who has not forgotten how to play or to be in touch with his or her own infantile self.

To Renata, a dog was not only a good object or an idealised "dog-god"[3]—a "mirror" play on words suggested by Bion. A dog, for her, was also the infantile mask of a person who can play with her.

After a pause, Renata said: "Dogs can communicate without using words."

"They're good at smelling; they feel." I added, touching my nose. "When they scratch a part of their body, they must feel something."

"They can have lice," she interjected.

"Something parasitic but alive in them?" I asked, keeping in mind the scratching of her dead body at the beginning of the session.

"I feel alive at night," she said, "when I go to listen to music at discos."

She paused and reflected:

"I used to like to paint and to draw. I used to draw quite a lot as a child," she said nostalgically.

"Would you like to tell me something through a drawing?"

I offered her a piece of paper and some coloured pencils. She chose only the dark-coloured ones. I had the impression that she wanted to express in her drawing something that she could not put into words.

She drew a tree, a lonely sad tree. When I asked her about it, she said:

"The tree is sad. It has neither leaves nor fruit. It is sad and lonely."

"What about the roots?" I asked her.

"It is a well-rooted tree," she answered.

Looking at the drawing, I had my doubts. It seemed to me that this stiff, melancholic tree was not as well rooted as she thought. Rather, I had the impression that the tree was standing on a surface like a piece of furniture. It resembled a table or a chair in the shape of a tree with its legs "standing on" the earth, rather than being "rooted in" the soil. I felt that she wanted to see herself rooted in life, alive, and fruitful, feeling the living landscape.

Then she drew a moth which gave me the impression of being flat and mechanically designed.

A long, pregnant silence ensued, in which I felt that Renata was trying to think and to remember something. As there were two circular marks on the wings, I asked her what they were. She was able to associate to them:

"They are like two holes, perhaps two round wombs." I found the expression "two round wombs" somewhat strange, but it made sense later on, as we shall see.

She continued: "One is an old, painful hole in my life. When I was around six or seven years old, I used to play with a boy of my own age. We got on very well together. He was like my brother, a twin brother. One day he left the village with his family and went far away. After that, I became very sad and withdrawn. In fact, it took me many years to overcome that painful loss."

She went on to tell me about the time when her mother was pregnant with her and her father had wanted a boy. I thought that what Renata had lost at birth and then as a small child was her "good" double, her masculine self. The description of the boy, who stood for her masculine side, was a picture of a lively and playful part of herself. Her painful mourning process, as Melanie Klein suggests, was not only due to the loss of an object, but also the loss of an object relation and therefore a precious part of her own ego.

When I asked her about the second hole in her life, she said that it had happened much later in life when she was twenty and found herself pregnant.

"I was mixed up. I wanted this child, perhaps a boy. But I felt frightened and unable to cope with the situation. Finally I had an abortion. My mother and sister knew about it but did not tell my father. They were too afraid to tell him."

"And you have felt cut off from life ever since?"

"Yes," was all she said in reply.

I saw her again a third time. She was very angry when she arrived for the appointment, because her boyfriend had decided not to take her out to the disco but to go out with his male friends.

"I was crying the whole day; it was as though he took something away from me." Then she spoke again about the abortion and associated to the good lively boy in her childhood who was taken away from her (aborted from her life).

I asked, out of curiosity, if she had seen this boy again. She was reluctant to answer, but after a while she told me that she had, in fact, seen him again when they were both twenty years old. It was an important event in her life, but unfortunately became a disappointing and painful one.

"He was not the same child whom I had kept alive in my mind. He was cold towards me and he did not remember the happy times we played together."

This was a tremendous shock to her. It was like losing him for the second time—and this time, forever. It was as if he had aborted himself from her life and left inside her a big hole, a void, a painful feeling of loss.

At that point, the image of the patient called Basilio came as a vivid *interference-cum-association* into my mind. In this way, in my mind, Basilio (whose treatment, still on-going, has been very successful) could also stand for the lively boy-part of herself. I would argue that, in Renata's mind, her former friend personified the illusion of restoring or curing the degraded and disappointingly cold image of her idealised boy-part when she met him again. The illusion of restoring the playful boy-part of herself coincides, in my view, with the family's romantic idealisation of my capacity to repair/restore Renata. Helping Renata implied for me, in my counter-transference, the realisation of her personal myth of bringing together and reuniting the lost male playful part and her female infantile part, just as in the Greek myth of the divine Androgynous.[4] Perhaps, in her romantic role of a sad, nostalgic moth wandering through the discos at night, she was searching for the idealised lost object and object relation. The wandering moth was also a wandering womb trying to find its place or the right "locus" to give birth to or find again (rebirth) the beloved hero.

I experienced in the transference her fantasy of the reunion with her lost object relation when I became her little boy-dog playing with the little girl-dog part of herself. Playing together meant finding the lost link or building a new ludic link.

The problem was how to relate Renata's mind or fantasies with my mind through an understanding of the "double" transference exchange relationship that was taking place both between us and also inside my own mental apparatus.

Renata spoke again about her temper tantrum at home when her present boyfriend let her down. She then looked at me inquisitively and said:

"Were you expecting me to come?"

"Yes, I was waiting for you to come to my disco," I replied.

And when I said disco I was thinking not only of her discotheque, but of the way in which my mind was the right "disc"—recording and understanding what was going on in her mind.

"It takes two to tango," I thought to myself. However, to be the right couple, one needs to dance together for a long period of time and to feel the same rhythm. The psychoanalytic process takes time and understanding, as well as the knowledge of the optimal distance in each transference. When life is monotonous and sad, the musical background is melancholic—a slow, heavy rhythm becoming a repetitive record always playing the same monotonous, lethargic melody. "Why did I lose my boyfriend, my little boyfriend, my lively 'Me'?" seems to be Renata's song as an echo in my mind.

Renata looked at the couch and asked me if she could lie down. "Yes, indeed," I said.

She lay down and became stiff and silent. I was trying to listen and to understand her dense silence. I felt that, at the very moment I was trying to listen to her, she was listening to somebody else. I communicated this thought to her and she responded by saying:

"Yes, in fact I am listening to somebody talking in my mind, somebody very critical and nasty. He always says 'No' to everything that I think or do."

I asked what sort of a person was this voice. She answered saying that it was a boy of her own age.

I related this superego critical voice to her beloved friend, or her beloved child part, which she had lost. The fact that when she met him again later in life he was disappointingly cold and nasty had "materialised" itself as a hallucinated voice in her mind. I knew that she was hungry for affection and jealous of her older sister's relationship with her father. I could imagine that she projected these feelings into the voice, which in fact could not tolerate a new link with someone else—in this case with me as the analyst.

I knew then that to propose a formal psychoanalytical setting to her directly would be difficult at this point. Although she wanted analysis, she knew at the same time that the voice, in another part of herself, was saying "No", hence her ambivalent or rather di-valent feelings (a term used by E. Pichon-Rivière).

It seemed that she was herself thinking about this problem because she said:

"I would like to be cured like that boy whom you treated. At home, nobody understands me and nobody can help me. Do you think that I need to be hospitalised, like the other boy?"

I thought about her recovery, but I preferred to wait. I know that psychotic patients in particular tend to test the analyst (as I suggested before) in order to know if the analyst's mind is the right container or the good "hospital". She also needed a psychoanalytic mental space where she could project or split off bad, stressful, persecuting feelings. She was trying to project not only persecuting or depressing feelings, but also good living aspects that she could not preserve within her own mind. Sometimes patients need to separate the good and bad aspects inside or outside of themselves in order to prevent them from being contaminated. Inasmuch as Renata felt unable to preserve the good aspects of her personality, she needed a "subsidiary" psychoanalytic body or a good hospital to keep them safe. The subsidiary body or maternal function needs to be completed by an organising, paternal subsidiary ego.[5]

During the next session, she again lay down on the couch and said: "The voice is now accusing me for having had the abortion." Then she added: "Oh, I've just remembered a dream that I had about two girl friends, whom I lost when I was fourteen."

"How did you lose them?" I asked.

"Well, they were angry with me, and gave me the cold shoulder."

She paused and added: "I know that I wasn't always very nice towards them. I tended to be extremely possessive and stubborn. So they obviously wanted to get rid of me."

"And the dream?"

"Well actually, I don't know if it was a real dream or if I was just sleepily thinking about it in bed."

What the patient called a dream was in fact an oneiric vision of her thoughts, which had been dramatised in the transference.

Who were the two girlfriends who gave her the "cold shoulder" during the session? One of the girls was the jealous or envious part of herself who was in opposition to the transference link, and whom she projected into the contradictory voice saying "No". The other was probably her own frightened self, her little scared girl-part apprehensive of this new experience. To become close to someone—me in this case—could also entail the danger of being abandoned or "aborted" at the end of each session or after a long separation such as the approaching Christmas holiday. In this case, it would be me who would be giving her the "cold shoulder".

In the fifth session Renata wanted to do another drawing. She drew three geometrical figures with a dark pencil: a pyramid, a cube, and a hexahedron with a rectangular base. The three objects, or characters, were inside a three-walled room; there was no ceiling, and the room was open to the audience like a theatre stage. I could see them as three geometric, "futuristic" actors, standing close together trying to relate, but not necessarily communicating amongst themselves. The curious thing was that the shadows were on the front surface of the geometric figures. It made me think about shadowy imaginary companions: in this case three people—the boy who abandoned her, and the two girls who gave her the cold shoulder. From the point of view of her mental space, they represented three internal objects or thoughts that were trying to connect with each other and were showing their sad, shadowy sides.

The open stage represented her mind opening up towards me, but also her geometrical, rigid way of thinking. When I communicated this to her, she replied: "I am thinking at this moment about a pyramid in a desert. I am also thinking about camels and nomads in the desert. Sometimes I think I'd like to be alone there."

"It's strange," I said to her, "just as you are about to open your mind to me, and to show me what is going on inside your intimate stage, another part of you separates from the other two figures and becomes like a nomadic pyramid and part of another landscape. I can imagine the other two figures changing into camels carrying your heavy baggage."

"I don't always like to relate to people," she said, and went to lie down on the couch.

Sitting opposite me and showing me directly what was happening in her inner stage was too risky. By lying down, she could be more relaxed, and she wanted also to hide herself from my direct gaze. However, since she could no longer see me, she felt isolated and started to talk again about her feelings of loneliness.

She was dramatising a split in her mind: on the one hand wanting to open out her stage and to communicate, and on the other wanting to escape into the desert: to desert me.

She became aware that in her deserting mood, her life was often dark and rigidly difficult. She told me several times that she tended to "square up" and be stiff and stubborn and remain immobile like the geometrical figures in her drawing. It also meant to me that her internal objects or inner actors were often static—or perhaps on strike.

How was I to link or relate together Renata's two images: the open geometric stage and the deserted one? I felt that Renata was facing a conflict between two states of mind: being e-motional or a-motional. The static actors stood for a paralysing of affective motion; an a-motional[6] state. When the actors, "players" or internal objects come alive, when they open up and move and become "moving", then the infantile self, the playing part, is reborn. But were this to be the case, she would have to pay the price of feeling and suffering: the price of living. To enjoy life is not always permitted; it depends on the superego and the environmental circumstances. For a fragile, sensitive ego such as Renata's, to experience feelings of pain, and perhaps joy, was much more than she could bear.

In fact, she was suffering from profound grief, part of an old painful hole and/or a disturbing mourning process. The two big holes or wounds in her life were related to two important object losses: her "real-imaginary companion" from childhood (who stood also for the lively boy-part of herself) and the abortion at twenty, when she became "formally" ill.

She became ill when she turned twenty, but her parents and sister described her as always having been very withdrawn and secretive. She used to be very attached to her father but at the same time frightened of him. She described him as being attractive and violent at the same time. She remembered scenes as a little girl, when her father used to spank her and her mother remained immobile, unable to intervene. Apparently the mother was also frightened of and dependent on the father. This nightmare image remained in her mind. She confessed to always having been scared of her father and, as a result, of men in general. On the other hand, she was nostalgic about the playful, idealised boy-part of herself.

I saw her life as an Odyssey in which she tried to "reunite" the female and the male parts of herself as an expression of her personal androgynous unconscious myth. I felt that my role consisted in helping her to travel through her nomadic quest, in opposition to her static and sometimes stubborn way of being. Hesitating between immobility and mobility, she had to deal with a double conception of life: on the one hand to avoid suffering and joy, to stop feeling, to be a-motional and apathetic, and on the other to return to life and to become emotionally alive again.

I am still treating Renata, and I find that sometimes her resistance and her immobility is stronger than her wish to "move" inwardly and to experience feelings. From time to time, the hallucinated male voice emerges and tries to occupy her mental space, filling it with his resounding "no". His systematic opposition does not leave enough space for her female part, who still says "yes" to psychoanalytic help. She wants to understand what is going on in her mind and to be helped, but she is afraid of suffering. Her old wounds (holes), which are now more sensitive, less dormant and therefore more painful, are more open to analysis. She is still afraid of being in touch with her old scars. She is afraid of her "coagulated" mourning process which, should it be awakened, could become rivers of blood. Mental bleeding is an expression of threatening, uncontrollable affective motion, strong e-motions, and frenetic drives. When insensibility and anaesthesia (feeling dead) are removed, sensitivity and pain are difficult experiences to bear—yet they are inherent to the very meaning of life.

During our most recent sessions, the playful, infantile aspect of the patient has come more to the fore. Through the infantile transference, the delusional aspects have become more and more accessible to analysis. Renata is, therefore, less blocked and able to experience, from time to time, moments of joy and to express some humour. There is therefore some life-sustaining hope able to react against the persecuting voice that prevents her from "mobilising" her coagulated wounded feelings. This is the way that Renata's girl-part and boy-part try to relate and play together during the transference situation like "in the old days". When the idealised playful boy-part of herself turned into a deflated, disappointing object (the encounter with her childhood boyfriend), it became a persecuting, hallucinated figure—a criticising hallucinated voice trying to put an end to her analysis.

## From mind to mind

The point I want to emphasise concerning the mind of the psychoanalyst and the mind of the patient is that being able to play or to experience a playful transference was an essential component of our work.

Analysts must be in touch with their own infantile self, the child within them—their child-part which has not forgotten how to play.

I would like to add a few words about my own analytic mind.

As I was imagining Renata's desert existence "in front of me", I kept in the "back of my mind" the image of Basilio—our "imaginary companion" and mediator. She came to me asking to find in her the lost, playful boy-part, the part she had loved and idealised in her childhood. The lost object of her childhood (into which she had projected a part of her ego) had changed and had become a persecuting figure after the painful reality-testing when she met him later in life, and he did not correspond to her expectations.

I understood during the sessions that Basilio, her "imaginary twin", was supposed to be the container for the boy-part of herself that she was trying to re-discover, repair and cure. This latter figure also represented in her mind the "good boy" part, which had played such an important role in the golden times of her childhood.

There was, as it were, an imaginary encounter in my mind between some of Renata's material and some of Basilio's; I would like to describe a dream that Basilio reported to me during the period that I was treating Renata.

Basilio's dream was as follows:

He was watching a television documentary film about China. It showed a desert landscape with no vegetation or houses. As the film continued, he was able to see some empty castles in the landscape. The castles sometimes seemed to be empty or to consist simply of two-dimensional façades. He added afterwards the word "geometrical" to the description of the castles and associated it to the neoplastic geometric painting that he had seen in my waiting room. As he continued watching the film, the nature of the landscape changed. Some vegetation appeared and he was able to see, in the distance, a group of inhabited houses with smoke coming out of the chimneys. All of a sudden, he was no longer a spectator of the TV film, but became part of the scenario. Thereupon everything became real, and he was alive in a living, real landscape. He was quite happy to be no longer emotionally blocked but alive, experiencing people, houses, and nature in their own reality. He continued walking and arrived at a marsh that had been transformed into fertile ground. He discovered some strange-looking frogs and tadpoles eating small mussels in a pond. In this fairy tale atmosphere, Basilio was very happy and, feeling very clever, he decided to eat the tadpoles that had eaten the mussels. He was very pleased with himself and playful in transmitting the fairy tale atmosphere.

In this dream, I was impressed by the word "geometrical" and the lack of vegetation, which reminded me of Renata's geometric drawings and her flat, bi-dimensional tree without roots. I was perhaps comparing in my own mental space two patients' minds, which were for me inter-related.

Basilio's dream was telling me something important concerning the progress of a psychotic patient in analysis. The dream was showing us that he was becoming aware of his developmental transformations during the analysis. In the dream, he became aware of the passing of time and how the flat, rigid, geometrical internal-object parts of his sterile landscape had changed through the analytical process into a living time appearing spatially as a fertile, playful, colourful picture.

The dramatisation of Basilio's dream describes his progress, his positive transformations during the treatment. From a sterile and barren state, which is part of a desert-like illusion ("false, flat castles in the air"), everything becomes inhabited by his own feelings and playful internal objects in the real and joyful context of his own inner world.

I thought "in the front of my mind", as I was looking at Renata's material and comparing it with Basilio's "in the back of my mind" (through an inner perspective), that if everything goes well in Renata's analysis, I will be able to help her as I did with Basilio.

In my mind I was connecting Renata (as a girl-part) with Basilio (as an idealised boy-part). In her mind, I felt that she was also trying to reunite this boy-part (also personified by Basilio—the reader will recall that she was referred to me by Basilio's parents—so, although she did not know him directly, she knew *of* him) with her infantile girl part in order to recreate the golden age of her childhood. On the other hand, it was important that I should not make any confusion between my mind and those of Renata and Basilio. This is one of the problems in our work concerning counter-transference and transference. We must be careful not to mix up two histories, which have some seemingly common aspects and features, but always remain specific to the individual as such.

It seems to me that the mourning process in Renata's mind was also introjected by me in my counter-transference. In my "psychoanalytic ego", Basilio stood for an anticipatory or wishful desire for Renata's therapeutic future. All these pictures are part of my past-present memories concerning my patients and my personal experiences in life, in which my own childhood and infantile fairy tale fantasies come together to complete my transference experience. I believe that we psychoanalysts do not react only as professional people to the patients in the classic sense of counter-transference, but sometimes also as "experienced patients" (by that I mean that we are in touch with our own personal analysis and therefore with our own ego-patient part) and most importantly, in a wider sense, as persons. What transpires between the patient and me, the psychoanalyst, is a confrontation and exchange or "inner transference" between two entities—the patient part of each of us and the analytical one (the intra-transference situation in its involvement with the inter-transference situation).

I must confess that at the start of any psychoanalytic experience, especially with psychotic patients, I have to accept and understand that most of the unconscious language will be for me and for the patient like an unknown foreign language, the "Chinese" in Basilio's TV dream. For some time, we have to put up with feelings of not understanding Chinese pictographic signs and "sounds", until (as the psychoanalytic process develops) we can change "Chinese" into a more comprehensible language. It is at this point that we become better able to understand each other. Therefore, if all goes well, I will be able to understand and to help Renata, as I was able to do with Basilio and other patients.

All this implies that it is my responsibility to make use of my mental apparatus in order to understand those of others. In musical terms, our mental apparatus is like a delicate musical instrument, and therefore fragile—it needs care. In this case, we must conceive of our mind as a valuable instrument, which needs re-tuning from time to time. Our work during the transference requires us to recall our own training—and our own therapeutic experience as patients—and to be aware of the difficulty and responsibility entailed in helping people whose "mental instruments" have become tuneless, discordant or broken.

## Discussion

As a psychoanalyst who has worked for many years with psychotic patients, I try to transmit my experience of transference with respect not only to the mind of the patient but also to what is occurring spontaneously in my own mind.

The term counter-transference, as Freud pointed out, denotes the reaction of the psychoanalyst towards the patient's transference. Money-Kyrle (1956) speaks of normal and pathological counter-transference, a very useful concept. But what is normal counter-transference? Under what conditions can the mind be enriched or disturbed?

In this chapter, I study my own reactions towards a psychotic patient who is able to observe intuitively (and therefore unconsciously) some of my attitudes in the transference situation. The patient was referred to me by the family of another patient who lived in the same area, and who had very much improved in the course of his analysis. During the psychoanalytic process certain aspects pertaining to this particular patient, and in particular a dream, came back into some "areas" of my mind. This was not an interference or distraction on my part, but rather an association "between minds" in my own inner landscape and led to a better understanding of the patient whom I discuss in some detail in this chapter.

The counter-transference feeling was a "syntonic musical experience" calling upon the different tones playing in the analytical mental space, with various melodies reverberating simultaneously. In order to communicate feelings or to give imaginary shape to the analyst's sensations, I need to make use of metaphors. Nietzsche himself used to say that words are not enough, and this is particularly true of psychotic patients. Besides, how else can we deal with associations which sometimes are confusing deviations but also may turn out to be enriching? Sometimes we should speak in terms of free *dis*-sociations in order to understand that there is indeed some meaning there. The psychotic mental apparatus is very vulnerable and sensitive, and also weak in its confrontation with the reality principle. Herman Nunberg's (1948) concept of ego strength and ego weakness is relevant here, and leads to the notion of the plasticity of the ego. Nunberg's paper was very much appreciated by Enrique Pichon-Rivière, who was my mentor in Argentina before my analysis in London with Herbert Rosenfeld, and who introduced me to the world of the psychotic. Perhaps one of the preconditions for dealing with psychotic patients is the capacity to tolerate, with flexibility, "distraction", some degree of confusion and intuitive sensations. The key is perhaps to put up with as much confusion as one can from the patient, and from one's own mind, and thereby go forth towards a new constructive awareness as part of the adventure which is the psychoanalytical process.

## Notes

1. The term psychosis is relatively modern and was created in 1850 by Ernest von Feminbersbaben in Vienna. Etymologically, psychosis comes from the Greek word *psykyhoem*, which means to animate. I find that psychotic patients often abandon unconsciously their own unbearable body in order to inhabit other objects or body egos and to animate them. This is related to the Greek and Oriental myth of *metempsykhosis*. The prefix *Meta* connotes the idea of beyond; after death, the psyche or the soul enters into another body.

2. Psychotics are mentally in pieces during the acute crisis and try to escape from their own body—they try to leave their own sinking ship, said Jaspers—and to enter other people's bodies, objects or things (projective identification) in order to be reborn again somewhere else (metempsychosis).

3. In Italian [the language that Renata and I were speaking], a frequently-used expression to defame or swear against God is *Dio cane* (God is a dog).

4. Plato speaks about the idea of Androgynous in his *Symposium* as the ideal reconciliation of two parts or two beings, one of which is masculine (*andros*) and the other feminine (*gyn*), who long to be reunited with each other and to grow together again.

5. One can also speak in terms of maternal and paternal *reverie*. Maternal reverie corresponds to Bion's (1962) description. But the notion of paternal reverie was suggested to me by Dr. Flavio Nosé (personal communication) from Verona as an organising and structuring paternal function in the transference.

6. The term "a-motional" (meaning without affective motion) is a neologism, which I created in my earlier writings in order to differentiate it from the term "e-motional".

# CHAPTER FOUR

# Bodily feelings in a dreaming world

*Clinical thoughts on psychosis and the infantile self*

Dreaming is a complex way of thinking; it is a particular experience in *oneiric* space and time, governed by what Freud called the "primary process". It therefore involves a very primitive experience in the unconscious. When Freud's book on dreams was published in 1900, it coincided with the mourning process he had to deal with after the recent death of his father. Like everyone else, he was unable to process certain aspects of this consciously, so he "closed his eyes" to reality and had a dream …. This was a normal kind of denial that operates with respect to any particularly painful experience.

In psychotic patients, feelings of loss and mourning processes are pathological. The psychotic ego is too fragile and sensitive; faced with a traumatic experience, psychotics tend to fall to pieces and to escape reality by running away into the world of dreams. It is as though they were bringing together the bits and pieces of their catastrophic reaction in order to construct a new vision of the world that has a closer relationship with an oneiric kind of "logical" thinking. In dream interpretation, the interpreter tries to find out the hidden meaning and hidden logic behind the dream.

Freud discovered through his work on dreams—in my view, his major contribution to the field of psychoanalysis—that the psychotic experience is similar to dreaming (though they are not, of course, identical). Also, the logic of dreams is sometimes comparable to the logics of the delusional world. In Freud's view, dreams can be a concise delusional prophecy. In fact in the oneiromantist tradition in Greece, when a "patient" was woken up in the oneirodrome of Pergamum or Delphi, the God of Medicine, Aesculapius, would appear and speak in the first person saying: "The dream means ... such and such". That reminds me that in my own analysis with Herbert Rosenfeld, he would sometimes say to me: "Salomon, I think that your dream is saying ..." On such occasions, I felt that my analyst was Asklepious, one of the elements that inspired me in my book on dreams, *The Theatre of the Dream* (Resnik, 1987).

In my book *The Delusional Person* (Resnik, 2001), I argue that in this kind of person there is a tendency to fill up the terrible emptiness of a painful loss, projected into daily reality, with a dream-like panorama that takes up most of the space in inner and outer time-life.

Bion often said[1] that at times the psychotic patient finds it impossible to differentiate between sleeping and waking states. Sometimes I have the same feeling with respect to my own psychotic patients; mostly, however, I have the impression that they are living in a dream-world and that they find it impossible to wake up.

That is why, generally speaking, analysts believe that psychotic patients cannot dream—but to my mind they are in fact dreaming all of the time, though in a very particular way. However, just as with normal people, if they cannot wake up, they can never know they have been dreaming ...

As we know, Freud established a close connection between dreaming and mental illness (Freud 1900a: chapter I [H]); other authors, including Garcia Badaracco (1979a), also link dreaming and psychosis. Garcia Badaracco focuses on the relationship between dream-thoughts and psychotic regression, arguing that this may lead to a sort of fusion/confusion between inner and outer reality. He goes on to say that in delusional thinking—closely connected to oneiric thinking—the patient is trying not only to fabricate a new conception of the world or a new "true-ness" for him or herself, but also to impose it on the world in general. Like Freud, Garcia Badaracco believes in an intimate relationship between dreams and psychosis, and argues that in almost any phenomena we can find both neurotic and psychotic aspects. For my part, I have attempted (in my book *The Theatre of the Dream*) to establish a semiological differentiation between psychotic and neurotic dreams (Resnik, 1987, p. 135 ff).

## Dreams and psychosis

I would now like to explore the interpretation of dreams and their relationship to psychosis within the context of clinical psychoanalytical work, with particular emphasis on the semantics of the dreaming climate in the transference situation and its impact on the analyst's own unconscious. Sometimes the analyst feels caught up in the dream-cloud that aims to make the whole world fall asleep—and thereby forget the painful and persecutory experiences of life. Freud uses the expression *dream-life* to indicate that in his view there was a particular atmosphere surrounding the life of the psychotic.

In that seminal work, Freud argued that hallucinating is a physiologically normal phenomenon that takes place in dreams. He mentions Wundt, for whom dream-images were a kind of illusion arising from faint sense-impressions which never cease during sleep (Freud, 1900a, p. 88). Freud showed how "day's residues" participate in the dream material.

It is generally accepted that in the psychoses the boundaries between inner and outer are to some extent lost. Therefore, day residues, night residues and hallucinations are mixed together. The effect is that hallucinations seem to be entering into the outer world. To put it another way, a sort of oneiric ideology of life takes possession of normal reality.

Many psychotics, who would not accept the idea that they are hallucinating, would nonetheless agree with us if we said to them that we have the impression that they are asleep most of the time, even though their eyes may be open.

I would like now to illustrate and to develop some clinical and theoretical points with the help of material drawn from the analysis of a patient whom I shall call "Samuel".

## Charlemagne's horseman

"Madness is made of dreams," Samuel said to me one day.

Samuel began his analysis with me in 1997. He was twenty-five years old when I first met him—a handsome young man, but detached, aloof, and very tense. In my consulting-room, he remained silent. He stood before me and looked all around, as though he were living inside a dream and trying to envelop me in his dream-mantle; indeed, I felt as though I too were being drawn inside a dream-world, in which hallucinating would be a normal way of life. He moved his lips as though talking to someone else. In fact Samuel was hallucinating all the time, apparently addressing some ghostly beings or other persons all around him. When I said to him that I had the feeling we were not alone, he said nothing at first, then, after a few moments, he declared: "There are soldiers all around us, Charlemagne's soldiers." Then he spoke about a "dead horseman". Given that his manner of speaking was not very lively, I said to him that perhaps he was saying something about himself—something about not being very lively/alive. With his voice still monotonous in tone, he said: "The soldier died in a battle." I understood Samuel to mean some time during what for him were the Middle Ages.

I learned from his parents, whom I first saw alone—at that point, Samuel did not want to come out of his "shelter" (as he would call his house)—that his illness began more or less when he started his university studies in political science. At that time, he found it difficult to concentrate and study; ever since his childhood, he had been a very gentle and passive boy, somewhat introverted. While he was a student in another town far from where his parents lived, one of his close friends became very worried because Samuel would neither answer the phone nor open the door to anyone. His parents went to visit him. He did not answer their call—so that they began to think he was dead, had committed suicide or had run away. His father asked the emergency services to break down the door—but this would have required proper bureaucratic procedures in order for them to do so. The parents insisted when, suddenly, the door opened, and in a very cold manner Samuel said: "Hello", then promptly disappeared. Other friends later said they had seen him in Rome, dressed in rags and living like a drop-out, sleeping rough … Several months afterwards, he decided to phone home because he had run out of money. He was then seen by several psychiatrists, who prescribed medication and psychotherapy. But he hardly responded to any of these initial attempts at treatment.

Over time he became more and more out of reach, and his parents came to consult me in Paris (this was a few years after the initial events). I told them that I would see him, and that they should let him know that I had the impression he felt safe and protected at home; perhaps he would feel better "jumping on a plane" (i.e., inside a containing object) to come to Paris rather than just walking out of the door ... with the danger of feeling lost when he found himself out in the open. Later, I was to understand that, at that time in his delusional world, Samuel, among his many identificatory figures, was at times living inside one of his ancestors (a famous World War I pilot, who had been killed in the last days of the war by the notorious "Red Baron", the German fighter ace). When Samuel "became" this heroic figure, it was of course very dangerous for him to get on a plane—because the Red Baron might well kill him too. He therefore decided to travel to Paris by train from the Italian town where he lived. The container in this case had wheels rather than wings ...

He was able to leave home and to travel to Paris because he felt protected not only by his parents but also by his hallucinated/created soldiers (and, later, priests) who were like a cloak around him. Garcia Badaracco (1986) argues that the psychotic, in his or her multiple pathological identifications, cannot be a "person", he or she can only be a "character" in some drama or other. I would add that the psychotic can change the "character" he or she is playing by climbing into and then getting out of his or her body armour, depending on the circumstances prevalent at that point in the patient's life.

One day, I realised that Samuel's hallucinations were not three-dimensional but two-dimensional and flat. For several months he appeared to be asleep, speaking only to his hallucinated environment; from time to time he would wake up from his dream-mantle and see me in front of him.[2]

Samuel was grateful for my emotional interest in him. He came to one session carrying a poster of Che Guevara—he knew that I am of Argentinean origin. When he showed it to me, he looked at me in a very dominant manner, as if trying to paralyse me and change me into a flat poster. When I told him of this fantasy I had, he said that he felt he had the power to change me into a "flat" person and that he did not want to lose this capacity. On another occasion, he said: "I had a dream, I was a magician, a kind of card-reading fortune-teller." I understood him to mean that he was beginning to wake up. I interpreted that the magician seemed to be related to his capacity to change a three-dimensional world into a two-dimensional one. Later, it became obvious that we were all like a pack of playing cards that he could control—the flat soldiers surrounding him, Che Guevara and myself; Samuel was holding all the trumps.

He admired Charlemagne, King Arthur, and Che Guevara—but he was also in a silent state of war or competition with these idealised figures. When he changed them into cards or posters, he felt that he could control all the important people whom he both admired and feared.

He told me about what he called "an old dream", which gave me the impression that he was re-enacting a catastrophic psychotic experience from the past. In this "old dream", a train was running at a thousand kilometres an hour, and at one point it crashed—some carriages were destroyed, others crushed flat. After the crash, the passengers came out of the destroyed train, changed into flattened people, like mechanical, dead shadows or something out of a comic-strip. This catastrophic "memory", in which people and the surrounding world became flat, reminded me of the book *Flatland* by Edwin Abbott (1884). In it, the author describes a two-dimensional world inhabited by lines, triangles, squares, circles, polygons—all in a flat, geometrical kind of existence. Triangles represent the working classes, squares and pentagons are professional people, and the nobles are represented by polygons that tend towards infinity, whereupon they become circles and represent the clerics. Women are straight-line segments—very powerful and persecutory. In my view, Samuel's world was very like the one Abbott describes, with its geometrical "comic-strip" characters. Sometimes Samuel felt it impossible to bring these characters back to life—he himself was very depressed and cold, in a melancholic kind of flattened state of mind in which there was an almost complete absence of feelings. In fact, as I pointed out, he used to speak of himself as a flat, dead soldier who died many years ago—in what he called the Middle Ages, during a battle between Charlemagne and his enemies.

At that time, Samuel was unable to find a link between the catastrophic accident of the train and the catastrophic experience of "his" Middle Ages. He sometimes had other versions of his illness—such as that of being on the *Titanic* when it struck the iceberg. Both Samuel and his family considered him to be a cold and frozen person. Some years previously, he had had quite a "crash" in his life, when his uncle, a very rich man, promised to make Samuel a partner in his company—at which point he would have had "titanic" power. When the uncle then refused to give him such an important role, something broke in Samuel's mind and in his heart. He became split into two antagonistic forces—or, to put it another way, into two warring factions. The experience of being dead (like Charlemagne's soldier)—a death-like way of living—made him feel very inferior and depressed. This was a kind of cold depression—sadness without feelings—a pathetic image of himself. In order to avoid pain, he tried to freeze all feeling (Resnik, 2005). Also, he was frightened by the very idea of coming back to life, of having an "existing" body with live/lively feelings.

One day he said to me: "If you cannot save me, you should prac-tise euthanasia, do away with me, make me die completely." This dilemma between coming back to life and being entirely dead became an ontological impasse; for the moment Samuel was unable to find a middle way between extremely contradictory ideologies (a delusion is also a system of ideas) relating to life and death. How could he find a meeting-point, how were we to find a space between us to deal with the metaphysical problem of someone who felt himself to be part of the living dead?[3]

After several months of analysis, he became more awake and more alive. He would feel hungry after his sessions and always wanted to eat a hamburger in a local fast-food restaurant ... I interpreted that com-ing back to life was hard and very difficult to digest; by comparison, a hamburger was much easier ...

One day, he told me he had eaten a crêpe (a kind of flat pancake) instead of a hamburger and that he had felt ill; he associated to the word *crepare*—which in Italian means "to die". It was as though he had chosen a kind of "self-euthanasia" in order to solve the problem of feeling unable to experience life once more. He was ambivalent—or di-valent as Pichon-Rivière put it—about "biting" into life as if it were a hamburger or dying and being helped to die (the formal meaning of euthanasia), thereby doing away with all painful feelings. Melanie Klein spoke of access to the depressive position, in which splitting and opposing outlooks may come together in one way or another.

One day Samuel hallucinated that he was required to have sex in a public swimming pool with several people, both men and women, but that nobody was there—he then realised that it was a hallucination. This eroticisation of death-ness characterises what Herbert Rosenfeld used to call a delusional state in which feelings and thoughts become eroticised as a way of bringing back to life in a mechanically exciting way the patient's own dead body and feelings. I find in my experience as an analyst of psychotics that the fetishistic approach, in which there is an attempt to bring a dead object back to life, plays a very important role in the pathological eroticisation of the mind and of the body. In eroticised fetishism, it is as though a corpse could be brought back to life through masturbation or sexual arousal: a necrophilic fantasy.

In one session, the patient told me about putting his penis into the crater of Mount Vesuvius. I interpreted that in becoming more and more alive he was getting in touch with hitherto-constrained feelings and sensations, including sexual ones, and that this was like exciting the volcano inside himself in a provocative way; it was perhaps both frightening and exciting to think that the people destroyed at Pompeii might come back to life ... Thereupon, Samuel remembered that, having been an only child until he was five years of age, he had felt terribly distressed when his mother gave birth—or, put it more accurately in a certain sense, gave life—to his little brother. He recalled a dream that dated from that period: flat and transparent, he was walking down a flight of stairs made of stone. At the bottom of the stairs lay a revolver, and he knew he wanted to kill somebody—maybe even kill himself. It would be true to say that Samuel was very sad and distressed at that period in his childhood. With a kind of nostalgic bitterness, he recalled the toys he used to play with. One was a set of little bagpipes. In the analysis, these bagpipes—*cornamusa*, in Italian—were transformed into a kind of hallucination/criticism of his mother who, as he said, "had been absolutely everything" to him. In other words, Samuel experienced her as a *musa*/"Muse" who was nonetheless making a cuckold of him (*corna*/horned—the hornlike emblem of a cuckold) by becoming pregnant with his little brother.

Later in the analysis, Samuel said that the panorama/landscape around him had begun to change. He felt less "flat", but other people seemed to be turning into matrioshka dolls, one inside the other. This made him think of the fact that he was paralysing his own feelings (matrioshka dolls cannot move); crying, for example, was an emotion he found alienating. Some months before he began treatment, his brother had died in a car accident; the car had skidded off the road and had crashed down into a ravine (the brother died in the accident—and was crushed/flattened under the falling car). In the session, Samuel said he wanted to light a candle for his little brother; his eyes reddened, and I thought he was about to cry. He told me that although the matrioshkas were sad, their tears were frozen ("Russia is a cold country", he added, "but I feel you to be a warm person"). My response was that Samuel was struggling between emptiness of feelings and coming back to life—he was therefore experiencing pleasure other than in a mechanically sexual way, which meant also that the ordinary unhappiness of life was coming into his "landscape" too. He was trying to exist again as a real, authentic person, not just as a "character" in some drama or other.

In one session, he made a drawing of the Arc-de-Triomphe in Paris (this is where the Tomb of the Unknown Soldier lies). He told me that he was struggling to know who was going to win—was it life, or was it death? The old/unknown soldier wanted—and at the same time did not want—to come back to life; so who was going to triumph? This is how I would put his question: the life instinct or the death instinct? Eros or Thanatos? They were like two armies in his mind, each with its rallying flag—the one calling for life, the other for death. Whenever I would ask Samuel a question, his answer (in Italian) would unfailingly be: *"Forse si, forse no!"* ("Maybe yes, maybe no"). I was able to interpret this as a struggle between two "forces/*forse*" inside himself. But perhaps they were now coming together somewhere inside his mental space? Was there to be an amnesty, an "understanding", a reconciliation between two split-off ideologies? The question was: how was Samuel to be himself again as one person? How could he get back inside his own skin? Indeed, the idea came to me that he was not even inside his own trousers—I had the impression that he was not "there", not "in" his trousers, but completely absent. This feeling led me to ask him what he was thinking of at that point. He replied: "I'm thinking of the TV advert for Levi's jeans"—which did indeed look as though they were empty: empty of life.

In the following session, he told me of a dream in which, as a writer of comedy, he was making people laugh. I felt that he was becoming a kind of Harlequin character serving two masters at the same time, as in Carlo Goldoni's comedy of that name—my associations were again to the *forse si* and *forse no* aspects about which he had spoken. I began to think that one of these was the master of magic and delusion, while the other was the master of the reality principle. I suggested that Samuel was thus changing from being a magician/card-flattening fortune-teller to a writer and then to a playful impish figure like Harlequin. With a smile on his face, he replied that he liked "underground" music; I suggested that the underground of his mind was a secret life that was beginning to come alive and to play: "I would like to be free and to visit the whole of France," he said. This made me think that Samuel was trying to escape from his prisons—I use the plural because I had the impression that in his schizophrenic world-view he felt scattered over several places and times. In order to return to being himself, he needed to liberate his imprisoned fragments that were dispersed over various landscapes.

The idea of foreclosure is perhaps a useful concept here. According to Lacan, in the schizophrenic experience, one of the origins of psychotic phenomena is what he called the primary repudiation of a fundamental signifier, that of the father figure or "name-of-the-father" (or, symbolically, the phallus). For Lacan, this repudiation (*Verwerfung* in Freud's words) takes place outside the individual's universe of symbols. According to Laplanche and Pontalis (1973) the signifier that is foreclosed is not integrated into the unconscious; it does not come back "from inside", but appears to be situated "outside", in the "real" world—and so is a hallucinatory phenomenon. In his seminal paper on the subject Lacan (1966) showed himself to be rather pessimistic as to the psychotic's ability to … climb back inside his own trousers, if I may put it so. My own experience, however, is quite different. As I see it, the phallic position keeps ego parts and the object world together. The analyst has to become an archaeologist trying to discover, with the patient's help, in what part of the landscape of the inner and outer worlds the exploding ego or father-function buried the fragments—for it is only then that we will know where they have to be exhumed from. The question/quest then becomes: into what "reality" or "character" or historical period were they hidden or masked?

In my work with Samuel, I associated to an inner army ("*forse si, forse no*"—positive and negative) hidden projectively (*Verwerfung*) somewhere in the woods, as in Shakespeare's *Macbeth*—with its concomitant change to "reality". I then had to ask myself how a hallucinated fragment could become a tree-army and change its nature … .

Thanks to his efforts to come back from dispersion and dissemination in a hidden, camouflaged world, Samuel gradually managed to return to his own body; less of a "character", he became more of a "person". He was slowly waking up from his dream-world. One day, he arrived early for his session. He was waiting for me at the street door, smoking a cigarette, all the time looking at his surroundings as though their novelty was something of a surprise for him. Once inside my consulting-room, I told him that this was the impression that I had

had on meeting him. He acknowledged this, and added that he felt he was waking up as though from a long sleep. He said also that recently he had begun to smoke heavily. I interpreted that his struggle was between the two philosophies of life that he was holding in his mind. He could either wake up and come back to life in a non-catastrophic, non-volcanic way—or he could puff clouds of smoke that resembled the dream-clouds in which we both had felt enveloped at the beginning of the analysis; he had all the same to recognise that these were becoming more and more evanescent.

The struggle between awakening to life and becoming excitedly euphoric was expressed in the sessions via his giving me a new "explanation" of his madness—which was no more or less than a new delusional hypothesis. I was struck by this "war" between the two phenomena—was Samuel to wake up or to go on producing smoke-like dreams? He was producing what appeared to be a never-ending "smoke-screen", a series of inconsistent delusions in which he himself did not believe. This existential struggle was dramatic, for he had to come to grips with both the sense of sanity and the sense of madness.

Now that he was aware of the danger, Samuel was terrified that he might remain a prisoner of his own dreams/delusions forever. Yet at the same time, the idea of coming back to life and finding himself a prisoner of his fiery emotions was also extremely disturbing.

For me, sanity implies that the projective-identificatory fragmented parts of the self, scattered over the multitude of waking or dreaming landscapes that constitute our minds, must at last be brought home. In my view, this is the only way that we can become ourselves again. We therefore need a genuine introjection that goes beyond the inner and outer struggles of our minds, in order to help us tolerate the different and contradictory narcissistic models of thinking and translate them into inner and outer dialogue.

I know that in itself this is not enough. In our work with our patients, it is not simply a question of "understanding" in some abstract sense of the word—we have to *comprehend* how their thinking began *to decompose* (Maine de Biran, 1824), in order to help them *recompose it* …. In one unforgettable session, Samuel said to me: "You know, in times gone by, my hallucinations really were thoughts." Through time, these thoughts had turned into hallucinations and smoke-screens; thanks to the analysis, they began to reintegrate his mental space (Resnik, 1995) and his inner experienced time (*temps vecu*, as Bergson called it). The work of the transference, as a kind of field-work undertaken jointly by patient and analyst, had to deal with an earlier breakdown in experiential time and space. As Freud noted (1937d), our task was to restore or to reconstruct, through the analysis of the transference, a world that, like Pompeii, had been buried for so long under layers of petrified, frozen lava, a world that we were about to exhume and bring back to life (this metaphor was suggested to me by Frances Tustin some time ago in a personal communication concerning autistic children).

I am grateful to Melanie Klein, to Herbert Rosenfeld, to Wilfred Bion, to Donald W. Winnicott, and to Enrique Pichon-Rivière who taught me so much, and to my wife Ana (also a psychoanalyst, and who often discusses my papers with me) for helping me formulate some of these complex hypotheses concerning sanity and madness.

If the therapeutic process works properly, the dream-world can change from a pathological and delusional world of near-death into a stimulating and creative one.

I am convinced that healing the psychotic experience makes us more aware of the creative processes that we see at work in talented artists. In motivated and gifted people, psychoanalysis is also an art, a work of artistic craftsmanship.

## Notes

1. In my personal supervision with him, as well as in many of his writings.
2. A patient of mine, whom I describe in my book *The Delusional Person*, suffered from schizophrenia. I treated her during the time I spent in London. On leaving one session, after some six months of analysis, she said that it was the first time that I remained behind in the consulting room-space. Up until then, she had believed that she could take me away with her, because I became part of her dream-world whenever she left my consulting room.
3. In my paper "The frozen man" (Resnik, 2001), I develop this aspect of the question.

# CHAPTER FIVE

# "No" in hysteria*

## *Freud on hysteria*

From October 1885 to February 1886, Freud worked at the Salpêtriere clinic in Paris under Charcot. Freud was very impressed by Charcot's Tuesday lectures during which he presented, among other patients, the fascinating, seductive and hysterical "Blanche". Freud was spellbound by Charcot/Blanche and by the impact of the hypnotic approach which allowed the patient to express herself. In fact, Blanche Wittmann, Charcot's "prima donna", had a double personality. Pierre Janet, one of those who attended the lectures, was interested in the splitting of her personality and he tended to think that Blanche Two was more balanced than Blanche One: perhaps a sort of inner rivalry?

Freud had already been impressed by Breuer's treatment of Fraulein Anna O. between 1880 and 1882. The treatment of Anna O. ended in June 1882, and in the following November, Breuer related the remarkable story to Freud, who found it extremely interesting.

---

*This chapter is based on an earlier article of mine (Resnik, 1992), which I have updated and to which I have made some significant changes.

When Freud arrived back in Vienna from Paris in 1886 and settled down to work with his patients, a large proportion of his clientele were hysterics. At that time, he was in the habit of recommending hydrotherapy, electrotherapy, massage, and the Weir Mitchell rest-cure. Freud, impressed by Charcot and by Dr. Liébeault from Nancy who worked in Bernheim's clinic, tried to make use of hypnosis with those patients. This method did not last long, however, because Freud soon realised that his personality was not sufficiently adapted to this method, in addition to other reasons that he discovered during the birth and early development of his psychoanalytic theory and practice.

Some years ago I was asked to write an article on hysteria for an important Italian encyclopaedia (the *Enciclopedia Einaudi*).

Hysterical phenomena were described in the Kahun papyrus (1900 BC) as a woman's illness provoked by the spontaneous displacement of the uterus, which behaves like a confused little animal wandering inside the body. The image of the "wandering uterus" corresponds to a very archaic fantasy which Hippocrates takes up in the chapter of his book entitled "Women's illnesses". It would seem that the fantasy of getting rid of such a disturbing internal object called "the uterus" and an early cathartic therapeutic method were intuitively suggested by the author when he stated that: "When a woman who is afflicted with hysteria, or who is in difficult labour, sneezes, it should be regarded as a good sign."

The word "hysteria", from the Latin *hystericus,* derives from the Greek *hysterikos,* the adjective of *hustera metra* and finally womb. In Latin *matrix* is related to *mater* and mother.

Theodore Thass-Thienemann (1967) speaks about a condensation of the Latin word *matrix* as a blending of *mater* and *nutrix.* One can therefore speak of hysteria as a disturbed wandering uterus-creature in difficulty. The mythical image of the devouring or consuming archaic mother and the Kleinian image of the greedy, crazy child inside the womb are interrelated. On one hand there is the fruitful, fertile and nourishing *nutrix* Mother (the Mother Earth who can also become angry—during an earthquake, for example) and, on the other, the picture of a swallowing animated "dead" womb, present in the word *sarcophagus* (which in Greek means flesh eater). I will come back to this topic later in this chapter.

At the end of 1886, Freud treated Miss Lucy R, a thirty-year-old Englishwoman working as a governess and living in the house of the managing director of a factory in Vienna. She was suffering from depression and fatigue and was tormented by subjective sensations of smell. She suffered also from a chronically recurrent suppurative rhinitis. Freud came to the conclusion that the obstinate persistence of her rhinitis was due to caries of the ethmoid bone. She located her "fatigue", her "heaviness" in her head. She lost her appetite and also her capacity to work. As regards hysterical symptoms, she presented a fairly definitive analgesia, especially in her nose. I gather from Freud's description that Miss Lucy was suffering from olfactory hallucinations.

Since Freud was interested in the concept of trauma at that time, he believed that these subjective smells, which were sometimes hallucinatory, had at one time been objective. When Freud asked her what sort of a smell she was hallucinating, she answered that it was a smell of burnt pudding. Freud assumed at that time that probably Miss Lucy had once experienced that smell in relation to some traumatic experience or other.

I would like to discuss some of those symptoms so clearly formulated by Freud. To put it briefly, she was a hysterical personality with strong conversion symptoms. The suppurative rhinitis in Miss Lucy is indicative of somatisation. The main difference between hypochondriasis and conversion symptoms lies in the fact that the former is experienced in terms of a "concrete body" which suffers a great deal without any physical or organic basis; what is denied is mentalization. In classical French psychiatry, hypochondriasis was looked upon as *a maladie imaginaire,* as if it were a delusional or hallucinated somatic experience. The actual conversion symptoms lead often to physiopathological changes which in turn sometimes give rise to "real" somatisation and organic disease. The field of psychosomatics has its origins in its relationship to conversion hysteria. We may therefore conclude that this young lady, Miss Lucy, was prone to a kind of exaggerated eroticism, or erotomaniac conversion tendencies, such as her nose being excited and experiencing, in bodily terms, a burning sensation associated with the burnt pudding.

As I said earlier, Freud at that time was attempting to discover a method that would be more suitable than hypnotism and somnambulism. He was thinking a great deal about free associations in cases of conversion hysteria. In addition, he wanted to discover the lost link between mind and body. He was very curious about the unconscious link that Miss Lucy could make between the "burning pudding" and a letter that she had received from her mother. When the letter arrived, the children that she was looking after stole it from her while they were playing. It was at that very moment that she actually did smell a pudding burning in the oven.

In reading Miss Lucy's case again, when I reached this particular point I associated to one of my own patients, Mr. B, whom I treated in 1960 when I was living in London and working at the Cassel Hospital. Mr. B was a man of about forty years old, very well-dressed, somewhat obsessional, and emotionally blocked, except for a particular isolated sensation, which became upsetting for him: it was the hallucinated smell of a burnt pudding. I was able to treat him for a few months but I could see no link between the symptom and his memories. One day I went to the cinema to see an English film. The main protagonist was a young woman of about seventeen years of age who became pregnant and did not want to tell her parents. She came from a modest, working-class background. Then a boy, her boyfriend or brother, I do not remember which, discovered this and said to her: "You have a pudding in your oven."

When I went back to my patient this expression was "burning in my mind", and I asked him if he could try to remember something concerning pregnancy. He fell silent and after a pause he recalled the birth of his younger brother, and how jealous and angry he had felt when experiencing burning feelings of hatred that he tried to suppress from his memory.

To return to Miss Lucy. I doubt if her contradictory feelings, or opposing affects as Freud puts it, were related simply to choosing between going back to England to meet her mother, and her attachment to the children in her care and her "deluded", eroticised love for the children's father. I agree that the nose element interested Freud who was influenced by Fliess's point of view (cf. his thesis on the nose) and, as we know, he was very concerned at that time with the idea of sexual trauma. The level at which Freud was conducting his therapy was related to the Oedipal/genital situation: Lucy was incestuously in love with a father figure, and of course fire (the burning pudding) had to do with sexual sensations. But from an Oedipal/Kleinian view, I was curious to learn about Lucy's infantile jealousies and whether she had sisters or brothers, probably because I made the association between her and my patient Mr. B.

Lucy's unconscious fantasies of burning hate or sending to hell the children who hid her mother's letter could be related to infantile memories concerning her family life. She could not tolerate any other child interfering with her relationship to her mother. On the other hand, the children stopping her from finding her mother's letter could represent parts of her own envious and jealous self related to the father figure.

In my fantasy about Freud's case, Lucy's symptoms were present in her early life and it was not only an attack on the children but also on the mother's womb/oven, pregnant with those children. Whenever I read an author who interests me as much as Freud, I have the feeling of establishing an inner dialogue with the writer.

Any reading, if one feels oneself really involved in it, becomes a dialogue with the text and at the same time a dialogue with one's own self, with one's own memory or, in my case, professional experience. Many years have elapsed since I first read Freud's early clinical papers but each time I read them I find new "suggestions".

Going back to Miss Lucy's unconscious fantasies, such as those which interfered with her own conscious fantasies, when the children hid or refused to give her the letter from her mother in Glasgow, she probably reacted in a "burning" violent way, which coincided perhaps with the strong smell of the burnt pudding: she was, in fact, at that time also burning with love for the children's attractive father. This in fact hid, through repression, the maternal-child oral level of relationship with her nostalgically beloved mother. Her nostalgic feelings appeared as a sensuous experience, an olfactory hallucinated memory simultaneously equated with the burnt pudding.

I am using my own fantasies and free associations concerning Freud's case of Miss Lucy and Mr. B still present in my mind. Any dialogue with the imaginary Freud becomes, through empathy and identification, an inner or "internalised" experience.

## Hysterical traits and the negative therapeutic reaction

In her book *Envy and Gratitude*, Melanie Klein (1975) makes some suggestions concerning the earliest emotional life of the infant, and the role of envy as an oral-sadistic and anal-sadistic expression of destructive impulses, operative according to her from the beginning of life, and with a constitutional basis.

Karl Abraham also speaks of envy as an oral trait and assumes that envy and hostility operate at a later period. Abraham (1955) does not mention gratitude but he sees generosity in terms of an oral feature. He considers that anal elements are important components in envy but stresses their derivation from oral-sadistic impulses.

Klein agrees with Abraham's views, but goes on to examine in some detail both the relationship and the difference between envy, greed and jealousy.

Envy, according to Melanie Klein, corresponds to the angry and destructive feelings aimed at any other person who possesses and enjoys something desirable. The envious person tries to take away the desired object, steal it, or spoil it. Envy says "no" to admiration and gratitude.

Klein goes on to argue that greed is an impetuous and insatiable craving exceeding both what the subject needs and what the object is able and willing to give. A greedy person unconsciously aims to scoop out, suck dry and devour the source of need: the breast. Greed is bound up with introjection and envy with projection. Greed cannot tolerate any "no" coming from the breast.

In Klein's view, jealousy is based on envy; it involves a relationship between at least two people, and is mainly concerned with love. But jealousy is a way of expressing the fact that the object of love has been taken away, like Lucy's mother's letter. Jealousy can also be seen as bearing witness to the fact that the individual is envious because another person is happier with a third party. In that case, the narcissistic wound tends to say "no" or to destroy the third party.

In some hysterical patients with strong schizoid tendencies, envy, greed, and jealousy are dramatised in a very theatrical and egocentric way. The patient in question usually becomes the director (*metteur en scene*) of the play, and can omnipotently distribute and impose roles upon the members of the cast. It is the inductive and effective projective identification upon other people which builds up a "no" or provokes a psychoanalytically negative therapeutic reaction. Freud himself spoke about "negative therapeutic reaction" (Freud, 1923b, p. 49):

> "There are certain people who behave in a quite peculiar fashion during the work of analysis. When one speaks hopefully to them or expresses satisfaction with the progress of the treatment, they show signs of discontent and their condition invariably becomes worse. One begins by regarding this as defiance and as an attempt to prove their superiority to the physician, but later one comes to take a deeper and juster view. One becomes convinced, not only

that such people cannot endure any praise or appreciation, but that
they react inversely to the progress of the treatment."

Fairbairn (1952) tries to draw a parallel between some regressive
aspects of hysterical patients and what Melanie Klein called the
schizoid position. Splitting of the ego, under a hysterical ego (apparently well-adapted to reality), can become successful in splitting the
environmental situation. Also it shows in a masterly way, and with a
great deal of satisfaction, the egocentric capacity for leadership. Hysterical power consists not only in being the master, the director of the
theatre company, but also in the capacity to get rid of unbearable anxiety into other people, through effective projective identification. On the
stage, it appears in the form of driving everybody crazy or guilty, as
I would like to show with the clinical case that I report in this chapter.

All this is related to infantile retaliations and painful or persecutory
experiences which the patient tries to split off and to act out in his or
her environmental situation. This is one way of avoiding taking on
board one's own mental pain and ego-splitting. Schizophrenic patients
are mainly split in their ego; they can upset other people very much
and frighten them, but they are unable to split the environment in a
hysterical-effective way. They lack a hysterical, strategic, defensively
strong ego.

Fairbairn suggests that many of Freud's earliest cases which I mention here were related to this relationship between hysteria and early
splitting of the ego. In order to understand endopsychic structure in
terms of object relationships, he suggests a revision of hysteria: back to
hysteria.

The idea of theatricality in hysteria is evident in Fairbairn's for-
mulation, when he treats internal objects as actors; as in the Venetian
Commedia dell'arte, Fairbairn's characters play classic roles. Harlequin
corresponds partly, in my view, to a "funny" hysterical and manipula-
tive inner saboteur. There is also an exciting object which could be an
exciting girl in the mind of Harlequin, which provokes him and drives
him crazy (like the feminine double of himself).

And then there is Pantalone, sometimes the father of the exciting
object, which stands for the classical super-ego (paternal super-ego).
There is also a rejecting object, which seems to me to take on also a critical punitive super-ego function, which sometimes may be maternal (the
maternal super-ego in Melanie Klein's work).

But perhaps we should see this living, theatrical image of the self as an expression of a living multiplicity of "beings" or objects or ego parts in the unconscious, in terms of an inner world. In that case, linking Fairbairn with Klein, one could say that hysterical splitting or dissociation between, on the one hand, cold or frigid feelings and, on the other, warm and hot or burning and exciting feelings should be understood in terms of sensuous object relationships. One can also say from a topographical and economic viewpoint that in each object there is implicitly a projected ego or superego part. As we know, for Melanie Klein, the paternal or maternal superego is also an object, which includes parts of the ego with specialised functions: sensuous, critical, but also guiding figures.

Following the concept of the maternal function (the containing mother) that we find in Klein, Winnicott, and Bion, I would like to add the importance of the paternal function in terms, for example, of a constructing, phallic and organising role in the endopsychic structure of the self.

Bion speaks about maternal reverie, the capacity of the mother (or the maternal aspect of the psychoanalyst in the transference) to take in unbearable, persecutory, and depressive feelings, which the infantile regressed self cannot "digest". Bion describes what he calls nameless dread. In my view, it is not enough to speak merely of maternal reverie, because the organising net of communications in the transference, and in each person's mind, is a connective experience, a linking paternal phenomenon.

In two of my papers on the function of the father, have I tried to differentiate maternal reverie from paternal reverie (this last concept was suggested to me by Dr. Flavio Nose, whose practice is in Verona, Italy). The containing function which Mrs Bick described in her paper on skin is not complete if we do not include the organising structuring function of the internalised father. I suggest also that if the combined parents in Klein's view are above all a persecutory bad combined couple in the infantile unconscious mind, this is due to the child's destructive projections onto the "bad couple" who abandoned the child in a hopeless situation. But beyond a "bad combination", we could imagine also a picture or a fantasy of the "good combined parents" in which the child can simultaneously introject the containing maternal function and the organising paternal one. This will be part of normal development when early persecutory fantasies are overcome.

For instance, when I commented, *supra*, on Lucy's hysterical and non-hysterical symptoms and linked them with my own counter-transference concerning Mr. B, I was implying that I created in my mind a "couple". My attempt to combine Lucy's burnt pudding in Freud's head with Mr. B's hallucinated burning cake in my own head—or perhaps combining Freud's and Klein's view in my own oven-mind—leads, I would argue, to a fertile combination. I am trying also to combine Fairbairn with Klein's view as a pregnant idea in my mind.

Hysterical narcissistic patients, such as those whom Fairbairn described, tend to speak a lot in the transference without taking into account other people's views or existence. In the transference the psychoanalyst can be denied. This mode of behaviour has the character of a narcissistic and omnipotent denial (disavowal or *Verleugnung*) of the other, and in a way a sort of tendency "to negate" (*verneinen*) other people's reality. Freud's paper "On negation" (*Die Verneinung*, 1925h), attempts to draw a distinction between negation (*Verneinung*) and disavowal (*Verleugnung*). The former is mainly unconscious, while the latter is more conscious. It becomes a repudiation by projection, a way of rejecting other people's views.

Sometimes the capacity to negate can be so strong from a sensory point of view that the perception can be eliminated: this is a negative hallucination. In some cases denial—an unconscious or conscious "no" to the object, to one's self or to other people—makes the inner or outer dialogue fail. In the transference situation communication is cut off and what sometimes remains is a pathetic mirroring soliloquy.

The capacity for denial, to say "no" to reality and to people's ego and object existence, goes together with a pathological gift for controlling and manipulating factual reality. In my first book published in France (*Personne et Psychose*, 1973), I used the term "induction" to describe the concrete capacity to induce other people (or the psychoanalyst in the transference situation) to respond unconsciously in a dependently reactive way to hysterical or psychopathic manipulation. It corresponds to a coinciding moment in time and space between "induction" and projective identification: a sort of simultaneous "acting" of the mind into another mind. The other person, unaware of the process of "mental acting" and induction, becomes controlled and therefore pathologically dependent.

Effective induction becomes an involving expansive imaginary "real" mantle like a toreador's red cloak. The transference field becomes the bullring where competition and fighting dominate the session. On the set (or scenery), split-off ego-observers (coming from both sides, psychoanalyst and patient) behave as curious witnesses, actors and spectators at the same time. Sometimes the egocentric expansive mantle behaves like a round, swallowing ego-mouth which eats up and devours time and space through seduction and hidden violence. The seductive hysterical side reminds me of what Charcot used to describe as *la belle indifference* in his patient, Blanche. As I write this chapter, I am looking at the photograph taken by Brouillet at the Salpetriere clinic in 1887. Professor Charcot is beside a very beautiful, attractive girl, probably Blanche, in a somnambulist, hypnotic, smiling state, with a very romantic seductive expression on her face. A man beside her, perhaps another psychiatrist, is "lovingly" holding her, and one can see all the others around her, including a female nurse, being excitedly attracted to and fascinated by this patient.

We can certainly value that strong, fascinating Blanche, trying to "involve" everybody inside her seductive, invisible, exciting and romantic mantle.

Between la *belle indifference* and her seductive attraction, we can "visualise" a major ego-split in that patient. Ego-splitting in the process of defence was studied in a very consistent and condensed way by Freud in 1938. That paper (Freud, 1940e [1938]) is certainly one of the most important of his later writings. I will add that, as it is unfinished, it leaves space for Melanie Klein's contributions on ego-splitting and on splitting of the object. Her paper "Notes on some schizoid mechanisms", read before the British Psycho-Analytical Society in 1946, could be seen as a complementary original investigation on splitting mechanisms of the ego as a "necessary" defence mechanism. I use the expression "necessary" because a fragile ego is not able to deal with inner and outer reality and with inner "bull-fighting" between objects and subjects; it needs to split them, sometimes in order to preserve a certain reality and to avoid a catastrophic, exciting encounter.

Integration can be experienced as catastrophic change (Bion).

Herbert Rosenfeld speaks about the "need for confusion" in order to avoid a traumatic necessary coming-together. This means also that confusion is a necessary step between splitting of the ego and bringing together part-objects, objects or different realities (1950b, p. 52).

To bring together split-off parts of the personality is a painful experience. It requires putting up with mental pain and being able to reconcile different objects and opposite feelings, as well as different views about reality, or different "reality principles".

Neurotic patients have problems concerning reality and have difficulties in negotiating between inner and outer reality.

Deluded patients will not negotiate with daily life and with formal reality principles. It is an "ontological principle" for them to create, to delude or to hallucinate a "new" reality. Neurotic patients are aware of having conflicts with reality and seek help with negotiating it. Psychotic patients and narcissistic personalities (many hysterical people are of this nature) do not want to negotiate; they want to change the human environment and to introduce a new physical and mental landscape. They demand that reality should be transformed according to their own wishes. For them, reality should be malleable, like clay, and should accept the model or form which is imposed by the deluded psychotic ego-sculptor. The matter of reality should react like Galatea to Pygmalion, becoming what the master wants or "to act" dependently, like a faithful slave. A formal reality principle is also at the mercy of the omnipotent egocentric ego of the narcissistic personality.

The narcissistic hysterical patient is gifted like a talented theatre director casting the various roles. This distribution of roles has to do with induction and mental acting to make people act according to "pretexts": the psychopathic hysterical patient is the ruler of the text; a text in which organising reality through manipulation becomes a powerful imposing disorganising ideology (as against the forming/formal reality principle).

Some psychotics cannot transform and control the environmental situation to the same extent as psychopaths or hysterical patients. As I have explained, using the theatre as a real metaphor, hysterical patients are often effective in upsetting people and making them act. It is not mere chance that theatrical attitudes and behaviour play such an important role in descriptions of hysteria.

As to the French notion of *folie hysterique*, I would add that Fairbairn's contribution regarding the schizoid aspects of hysteria helps us to understand psychoanalytically some of the psychotic aspects of regressive hysterical patients. Hysterical patients with powerful psychotic features tend to challenge reality with a huge "no". Denial and disavowal of other people's views can be very strong. At the same time, in the transference they can upset the psychoanalyst, who has to be very cautious in the counter-transference. The capacity for attacking the analyst's mental apparatus and upsetting him or her can be very pronounced and resourceful. This way of dealing with other people's minds can be a perverse source of admiration for some people, inner and outer (in hospitals, where competition between members of staff is very strong, or in certain families). Unconsciously, the narcissistic, challenging side of the patient is able to make the analyst lose control of the situation. All of this can arouse hatred or feelings of hopelessness in the transference and counter-transference.

Being analysed and making contact with one's inner world can sometimes become a dangerous and upsetting event. It can be like discovering an unknown monster submerged in the unconscious. The nightmare appears when the frightening monster emerges from the repressed waters of Loch Ness. Those feelings are equivalent to what Bion described as nameless dread.

According to Bion, normal development between infant and breast/mother allows the infant to project a dreaded feeling—for example, of death; something unthinkable for the child which we call death. The infant tends to get rid of these unbearable feelings by putting them into the mother. If this projection is not accepted or tolerated by the mother, they are reintrojected, and come back not only as a "tolerated fear" but as an intolerable nameless dread (Bion, 1967, p. 116).

The hidden monster of Loch Ness could personify the submerged mythological source of the nameless dread as something archaic, not yet born or not yet named.

If the patient discovers that the mantle is a false one and that the deluded system of ideas a mistaken one, he or she can become resentful and destructively violent (the Loch Ness monster comes out from the water-mantle and shows its mask). Sometimes patients may be extremely disappointed and deeply depressed, as though the idealised object, the deluded mantle, was losing its power and becoming a sort of deflated balloon. I call this phenomenon "deflation of the ego". Sometimes the destiny of the deluded inflated balloon is to burst out, to explode.

The pathological ego ideal, the inflated balloon, the idealised bull-fight mantle can become an expansive tissue or net which tends to take in, like a gladiator, all the objects (inner and outer) around or inside him. This megalomaniac expansion of the self can change into an archaic greedy monster. That expansive, greedy, ambitious, eating mouth of the monster eliminates any other identity and transforms the world into something nonsensical, a degraded picture of the real world. This view coincides with Herbert Rosenfeld's concept of catastrophic destructive narcissism which does not tolerate diversity, a concept based on Klein's analysis of envy (Klein, 1957, p. 176).

When delusion is seen to be a mistaken illusion, the patient is painfully disappointed and can become very violent towards other people—but above all towards him or herself. Such patients become angry when their deluded ideology is unmasked and proved to be inconsistent, only inflated, just air … The deluded ego-ideal, the balloon of the delusional propaganda changes into violent revenge or into hopeless depression.

Sandra, a hospitalised schizophrenic patient suffering from "etherotopic delusions" (which I understood as "heterotopic delusions"), started to suffer greatly when the etherotopic balloon began to deflate. I should explain that "etherotopic delusion" is the name the patient gave to her illness. According to her, she became ill when she started to feel enormous mental pain, up to the point where she decided to put her brain into a container full of ether. From this came the expression "etherotopic delusion".

Once she began to feel better from all points of view, which meant that she was able to experience feelings (she was a severely schizophrenic patient in a chronically blocked state), she became more hysterical, seductive and creative. She used to write wonderful poems. At a particular moment she started to blame the hospital, the director and myself, saying that her ether was being reduced. In fact, when the etherotopic balloon became deflated, her mental pain began to increase again. She therefore felt split into a disappointed picture of herself suffering unbearably, because of her need for free expansion. She felt ambivalent about "etherotopic therapeutic deflation" and "expansive growing etherotopic delusion". Her delusional self started to project hallucinated monsters on the ceiling trying to frighten and to control everybody from above.

Those monsters were frightening masks dramatising a powerful and thanatic pleasure, a sort of eroticisation of the death instinct opposing life. Eroticisation of fear and pain was, for Sandra, one way of challenging mental suffering.

Ronald Fairbairn (1952) has attempted to bring together several views concerning hysterical features in psychosis. He speaks about splitting of the ego and hysterical dissociation, highlighting Freud's earliest research on hysterical phenomena, and writes also about Abraham's and Melanie Klein's contributions to the understanding of the earliest stages of the Oedipus complex.

In his chapter "Back to hysteria", he describes hysterical schizophrenia and the early splitting of the ego. He relates splitting of the ego and of the object to his picture of "a multiplicity of egos": as in a dream, they are all parts or representations of the Self.

Fairbairn sees dreams as a short condensed meaningful film. In any case, if it is a film, it will be a three-dimensional one as in a theatre. The title of one of my own books, *The Theatre of the Dream* (1987), shows that I prefer the metaphor of the theatre stage in describing dreams, a stage where scenes change all the time, quickly or slowly (maniacally or depressively).

Being also very much attached to Venice, where I live part of the year, I have the image of dreams (or of a dynamic endopsychic structure of the mind, such as that pictured by Fairbairn) in terms of a Venetian pantomime. Looking at Fairbairn's diagram concerning the endopsychic structure of the Self as a living stage brings to my mind the *Commedia dell'arte* as a living metaphor for dreaming and thinking.

I have already given actor roles to Fairbairn's categories of the mind. One was Harlequin using the mask of the internal Saboteur, a sort of funny, charming, and envious creature. Sometimes he becomes a shamanic figure, a powerful, magic leader (a super-ego mask). On other occasions he will use the mask of the libidinal-ego. Then there is the exciting object which could be played by Beatrice, Valeria, Colombina, Lavinia or Isabella—all of them exciting figures, masks trying to seduce Harlequin in his fantasy. Then again there is the rejecting object which can be personified by Pantalone opposing Harlequin's desires or Brighella or the Capitano. There is also the central-ego or main part, which stands for the public (internal public): a multiplicity of ego parts looking at the stage without participating directly in what is taking place between the actors. According to Fairbairn, the central ego does not participate other than as a recording agent. Hence my image of an audience, either off-stage or on-stage: a Greek chorus.

I can see also Pantalone with his large maternal stomach as an archaic phallic mother with a funny child inside him—this could be seen as Melanie Klein's theatrical picture of early development.

Endopsychic dynamic structure in terms of Melanie Klein's and Fairbairn's views and the theatrical metaphor of the *Commedia dell'arte* should be completed by the image of a multiple and pluri-centred mental apparatus. This connects with Ignacio Matte Blanco's conception of the unconscious in terms of the plurality of the mind. He speaks of a dreamer who sees a multiple-dimensional world with eyes that usually see a three-dimensional world (1975, p. 418). According to Matte Blanco the notion of multiple dimensions was suggested by Freud himself in *The Interpretation of Dreams*. The ego-observer (or central-ego, in Fairbairn's terminology) appears in dreams in a split-off way by assuming different roles at one time: to see simultaneously the same thing from different perspectives. This is a way, according to Matte Blanco, of escaping the limitations imposed by three-dimensional space.

To return to Bion's nameless dread and maternal reverie (the capacity of the mother to tolerate the infant's dreadful projections, and to send back good metabolised transformations), I would like to draw the reader's attention to what I call paternal reverie, in order to complete the picture of an imaginary complex reality.

All of this is related to the qualitative transformation of the child's projections in the eyes of a combined maternal-paternal reverie, as I shall discuss later.

The idea of a maternal reverie able or not to contain the infant's dreadful or good *projections* is not in itself enough. Projections need not only to be received but also organised or helped, and this by means of paternal phallic support, the paternal function. Paternal reverie implies the capacity to deal with unstructured phenomena: changing an unvertebrated experience into an organised vertebrated one. It is as if the re-introjection into the Self of a paternal phallic function acts like a spinal cord helping to "vertebrate" the disorganised mental apparatus. Both maternal and paternal reverie are complementary in terms of a good, combined parental function.

Discussing hysteria and reading Breuer and Freud's papers on this subject imply a complex and fascinating wandering into past and present history. When I say history, I also mean my own history as a psychoanalyst, working for many years with neurotic and psychotic patients.

For a long time now—and it is still the case—I have been concerned with the application of psychoanalysis to difficult patients in general and psychotic patients in particular. Getting in touch with the earliest levels of the mind or with unconscious, repressed wishes and fears, related to exciting or upsetting and destructive fantasies, meant that

I was always very much involved in the transference. That sort of experience is a very difficult task but at the same time an enlightening one.

The patients who are most disturbing are not necessarily chronic schizophrenic patients or those presenting acute psychotic dissociative breakdowns, but patients of any sort who have strong paranoid and hysterical traits.

The main practical difference which I make is between actual schizophrenic patients, who do not act out very much or do so in an inefficient way, and borderline, psychotic or emotionally disturbed patients with strong hysterical tendencies, who do act out and manipulate reality in very efficient ways.

Several Kleinian analysts, in particular Herbert Rosenfeld, have worked on the psychopathology of narcissism and its relationship to what he calls "destructive narcissism": patients who act in the transference situation in a very disturbing and upsetting way. Those cases are related to what Freud described as negative therapeutic reaction. They feel hurt when they are being helped. This negative attitude, this "no" addressed to the therapist, is related to admiration and envy.

Melanie Klein has shown us that envious persons are egocentric beings who cannot stand admiring anybody but themselves. They always attack somebody whom they admire "enviously": instead of expressing gratitude they react destructively.

## A clinical illustration

Some years ago, a young twenty-five-year-old woman whom I shall call Sonia came to see me in Paris, referred to me by a colleague. She felt particularly distressed and not well adapted to reality ever since her French parents had moved from Turin in Italy back to Paris. She was born in France, and when she was a little child, her father, an engineer, had taken a very important job with a major corporation in Italy.

When she was twenty, her parents decided to come back to France, and ever since she had felt very disturbed and unable to adapt herself to the new situation. She became very aggressive and destructive, physically and verbally, mostly attacking and accusing her father. She made him feel responsible and guilty because he had once again changed countries.

She had always been a very sensitive girl, but irritable and sometimes unstable whenever her parents or somebody else failed to do what she wanted.

Sonia's mother described her daughter as being strong-willed, infantile, and sometimes obsessional. When she was a small child she would shut herself in her room when she was upset, rocking to and fro in an armchair or on her bed so violently that sometimes, when she was older, she would break the bed.

She has a younger brother, whom she tended to ignore completely, as though he did not exist. In fact, she behaved as if she were an only child, occupying through her behaviour and character the whole family space.

When she was frustrated, she used to react violently, as I have said, also upsetting her parents in a very effective way, such that they felt obliged to do what she wanted.

I saw her both on her own and with her parents, who spoke incessantly of her, as if all their problems were personified by and focussed on her (she was the "central-ego" of the family). Sometimes, Sonia attacked her father and was able to convince her mother that the father was mad and responsible for all her unhappiness. As I said before, the move from Italy to France aggravated her symptoms, her anxiety, and her violence. When I saw her, she often travelled by train to Turin to see her psychoanalyst, whom she continued to visit for some time. She did not feel well either in Turin or in Paris, only "in-between", as it were, when she was travelling on the train. This balancing between two cities was related to one of her main infantile symptoms: compulsive violent rocking.

I saw her precisely because she stopped going to her psychoanalyst at a particular point in time, but wanted to continue seeing a psychoanalyst here in Paris. I saw her for some time, a few months, and then she decided to go back to her analyst in Turin. I would like to take up some of her symptomatology and transference situations during her "acting in" and "acting out" with me, until I was able to help her to go back to her former analyst.

Her rocking symptom reminded me of some children with autism whom I used to treat years ago. What she was telling me during the first sessions was that she did not feel well either in Paris or in Turin. She felt well only when she was "rocking" in a motherly chair-train.

In one of her sessions, she told me again about her rocking and how she felt both excited and angry when she was doing that. I understood later, when she spoke to me about compulsive masturbation, that her mental and physical excitation was also eroticised and mixed up with very destructive and perverse phantasies. She described herself rocking until she became empty, or until she disappeared and became invisible. She said: "At night I see the shadows that are against me. Sometimes I feel myself being a shadow, angry with the other side of myself" (the light side). She confessed to me that she was frightened of her own violent feelings coming out of the darkness. Sometimes she felt that she was a victim of her own impulses, which she could not control. Then she told me that when she was holding a glass or a plate in her hands she would take fright in case some uncontrolled part of herself might throw it to the floor or break it.

She said to me once that she sometimes regarded herself as being fragile like a piece of glass or a fragment of broken glass. At a particular moment she looked at the window pane and said: "I know I am fragile like a piece of glass, but somebody crazy living inside me is pushing me to break myself. I sometimes feel like breaking the window and throwing myself out".

She explained to me that this fear of self-defenestration was so strong that she reacted with courage, deciding some years previously to become a parachutist. She took therefore a counter-phobic decision to throw herself into the open, protected, as I understood it, by an efficient "inflated skirt" (the parachute), in order to overcome her fear of falling down into the unknown: inside or outside herself.

In the transference, she was very curious and frightened at the same time, trying to look through an "inner window" inside herself, into her own mental space. She therefore had ambivalent feelings about being analysed and becoming dizzy and in danger of looking inside herself, which would turn out to be a bottomless abyss.

Going inside implied the risk of being tempted by her own curiosity and then falling down into the darkness.

Often she did not know what to do with her ambivalence and divalence, concerning two places, Paris and Turin, and between two tendencies: to glance into herself (equated with inner defenestration) or not to look inside herself. In the latter case, this would imply projecting her unbearable inner world outside, out into the open, into the world (through the window, through her eyes/windows).

Sometimes, she would speak and express herself with feeling, in a warm way, but at others in a detached and cold way. She was at times able to be affectionate, charming and seductive.

One day, during a session, she reported the following dream: she saw a low wall, on which a young child of seven was sitting. He was rocking back and forth, he did not know where to jump, which side of the wall to go. "I was that little boy," she said, "sitting or lying on the wall on the edge, the border: am I a borderline patient?" She laughed.

"When I was seven or nine, I don't remember exactly, I was in love with my uncle, I wanted to marry him. He married somebody else, a girl of the age that I am now, and that hurt me a lot." I understood from what she said to me and from the tone of her voice that when she was angry she became masculine, a boy.

She told me a second dream which took place in a clinic. "I was looking up at the wall at a water pipe. I think it was a plastic pipe. I don't know why that makes me think about my vagina, perhaps a plastic one. I feel sometimes that I am detached from my own vagina or that my vagina is detached from me."

Going back to "no" in hysteria and to my paper in the *Enciclopedia Einaudi*, I recall again the image of the "rebellious wandering womb" or perhaps of a detached wandering "plastic phallic vagina" (the pipe). The rebellious womb-pipe was tense and often in a state of erection, when Sonia wanted to be not a girl but a defiant boy.

I recall an image from more than forty years ago when I was in training at the Argentinean Institute of Psychoanalysis in Buenos Aires. On one occasion Professor Arnaldo Raskovsky, speaking at the institute about the myth of Salome, described her as a beautiful seductive phallic girl dancing, turning round her "erect body" (dancing on tip-toe) and meditating how to castrate, how to cut off Jean-Baptist's enviously admired head.

I found this image quite plastic and expressive concerning penis envy in women. Sonia admired the intelligence—and therefore the head—of her beloved uncle, just as she would admire my head when, according to her, I made some clever remark in the transference situation. On the other hand, she often felt narcissistically hurt when I tried to be helpful. She would speak about female and male psychoanalysts, saying that a woman would understand her emotionally and a man rationally. But I was able to tell her that she was talking also about two sides of herself. She was very upset because she thought that her (female) psychoanalyst in Turin was very sensitive and touching but in danger of being hurt and driven ill or mad by her violent feelings (her male part or her female phallic one).

Sonia talked of her phallic obsessions: she did not want to be just a girl with a feeble plastic vagina; she wanted to be big and strong like Samson, able to kill the Philistines. In fact, like many hysterical patients, she became a phallic Salome trying to frighten and castrate Salomon, i.e., me.

She would tell me that she was trying to frighten me as apparently she used to with her earlier female psychoanalyst. She felt that Samson (or Salome with her seduction) could kill me. She would express, as I have pointed out, some worry about that earlier psychoanalyst, because a woman is in more danger than a man. A woman is emotional and a man is rational and unemotional.

I understood that she was afraid of establishing a link with me as a mother figure because the Samson in her could destroy the good maternal reverie. In addition, her female phallic side (Salome) could destroy or disorganise the paternal reverie in the transference.

Sonia was afraid of her own drives and impulsions. Her hysterical womb or phallic vagina could become a dangerous bellicose weapon, changing the plastic tube into a revolver or a pistol. In fact when she became angry she would indeed shoot and fire at anybody.

She described herself also as a demon, an evil spirit, a devil who was proud of her own power ... The secondary gain of frightening and challenging anyone made her feel strong and powerful. She was proud of being an efficient diabolic antagonist and able to use with success her "frightening phallic pipe".

In another session she described herself as a suffocating figure, but sometimes she felt that she herself was being suffocated. She described that state of choking as a sort of oppression in her breast, as though her expansive *globus hystericus* was turning into a convulsive creature, a megalomaniac animal so inflated that everybody in the vicinity would be crushed ...

She would say: "I am a demon but also a little frightened girl."

In another session she again hallucinated the low wall of her earlier dream. She tried to make me hallucinate that wall also, saying that she felt that she was low and small and wanted to make me feel low and small like her. Thus she would not be hurt by heterosexuality, heterogeneity or anything else that could make her feel different and inferior.

She saw herself as losing contact with herself, and therefore becoming detached or depersonalised. Sometimes she described reality as something unreal or de-realised.

"I do not know what to do with myself," she said, "I don't know whether to go forward or backward …" She was telling me that she did not want to lose her status of someone sitting on the wall like Humpty Dumpty. Humpty Dumpty was driving Alice crazy. She wanted to know why that strange creature tried to impose on her his world of "glory". His intention was to use the phonetic matter "glory" as a shape for any other language, thereby imposing a delusional shape on the world.

In Lewis Carroll's text, Humpty Dumpty says, addressing Alice: "My name is the shape I am, and a good, handsome shape it is too." And he adds: "With a name like yours, you might be any shape almost" (1978, p. 263).

In one of her sessions Sonia started to rock to and fro, saying: "I am trying to rock out of time, I do not like sharing time, I want to impose my own time." Sonia, like many other borderline and psychotic patients with hysterical traits, did not want to share with me the time and the spatial frame of the session. Such patients want to dominate the psychoanalytic space and time, the formal setting.

Sometimes Sonia was able to see herself as a hard and cold person; she spoke about the congealing of her feelings. It was precisely when she became hard and cold like a piece of ice or like an iceberg (a cold frozen Samson) that she felt that she was about to fall down and break into pieces. This was the case also when she identified with a glass, a crystal or a mirror.

Sometimes she identified her masculine Self with an important figure such as Baudelaire, the great French poet, who was not understood in his time. Once she saw a photograph of Baudelaire (by Nadar); she found him nasty and perverse. When she said perverse, she had in mind a macabre picture of a skeleton.

Sometimes she thought about the countryside and the brown earth: "I think about a big hole in the earth and an abyss where I can fall down infinitely. Perhaps that was the reason I became a parachutist." During another session she spoke of the abyss and chaos as a big mouth which was going to swallow her.

On another occasion she said: "I am thinking about a scene from a Russian novel: I see two people duelling. One of them committed suicide before fighting, probably because he was afraid."

What came to my mind, in my counter-transference, was Sonia changing her phallic pipe into a sword or spade fighting with my "mental sword". She said that she was afraid of me and would then feel paralysed.

After a pause, she said that she was thinking about "Paris and Turin fighting in her mind". Sometimes the fight took place between a man and a woman.

She gave me to understand that sometimes the fight was between places or spaces, but at other moments between different times in her own life. She thought of herself as someone arrogant but also simple and weak, living in different times and probably in different spaces at the same time: "Sometimes I feel so powerful that nobody can stop me and nobody can contain me. My wish at that moment is to crush and smash everybody, any opponent, but then everything collapses and goes flat."

I understood that I had to be able to stop her and to contain her.

At the same time, she would say that she wanted to jump out of the window. In the transference, Sonia described herself as somebody who lost contact with her own body and with other people.

For some time Sonia would make use of her own "mental sword" as a means of "castration" in the transference, using her surgical gifts as against her need to communicate, attacking the link between herself and me.

I tried to show her how her mind was split, struggling either between the male and female parts of herself, or between accepting the fact that she was a patient and feeling offended and revengeful. In the transference, she acted out a catastrophic surgical weaning; what came out of her mind was a broken mouth or a mutilated breast.

As time passed, Sonia gradually became able to tolerate her own mental space. She was then able to gain insight into herself and become more able to tolerate her own internal abyss.

The phenomenon of manipulating both those close to her and the analyst in the transference situation was from time to time a powerful element.

At one particular moment she was unable to listen, and complained of having a great deal of pain in her left ear. She associated that suffering with a painful earache that she had when she was a child. Then she added: "Sometimes I feel that my left ear is asleep."

"I am thinking about my analysis in Turin with my female analyst. One day she said something hard and painful to me. It was as if she was making a hole in my head. I couldn't stand it. Perhaps she touched a painful wound in my mind." I thought about a painful psychoanalytic sword-thought getting into her mind.

She frequently complained about her father: "He drives me mad, he's cold, unemotional, and so rational, just like all men." I commented that she was projecting onto her father her own rational and cold male part.

"I would like to be a real woman," she once said—then suddenly felt a strong pain in her left ear. "It's like a nail being hammered into my ear." The transference situation could become so persecutory that talking to her, whether me or her former female analyst, became equated with a harmful, brutal nail; a raping voice getting into her mind. I understood then that my voice and my interpretations—like her own violent masculine voice—could turn into a harmful weapon. She was afraid of re-introjection, which meant for her completely losing her mind.

In the following sessions she fantasised about going back to her analyst in Turin, which I found rather positive. She had become less persecuted in the transference by the "archaic Kleinian phallic mother".

Sometimes she would be feminine and emotional but she did not like that very much. So once again she would become a violent man, a powerful and destructive Samson.

She was still aggressive with her parents at home who were very frightened of her. As it was very difficult to contain her at home, a psychiatrist who saw her got in touch with me and suggested that she should be hospitalised. On that occasion she said: "No, I am the strongest." When I told her that Samson was sometimes still strong, she smiled and changed suddenly saying, "I should hold back and control myself."

I understood that she would try to control herself (the inner paternal reverie) and go back to her female analyst in Turin. Three years later, she again left her Turin analyst and came back to me.

Here we were again with Sonia balancing between Turin and Paris, with her terribly ambivalent struggle between "yes" and "no".

I did not have any time available for her at that point, and asked her to wait.

I was during that impasse that I wrote this chapter, having in mind Herbert Rosenfeld's book, *Impasse and Interpretation* (1987), in which he speaks about difficult patients with tendencies towards negative therapeutic reactions and often strong hysterical features.

## Discussion

Some of the most interesting and difficult patients whom I have treated during my long professional life were those who presented major psychotic features allied to hysterical character traits and behaviour.

Freud from the very beginning was faced, as Breuer was, with very difficult hysterical patients with whom he was able to deal in a very gifted and intuitive way. In my view, Freud was a very flexible man, a very deep and original thinker with a great character, which allowed him to "fight" against his patients' manipulation.

Freud's legacy also helped me to understand the fact that hysterical patients or deeply disturbed psychotic or borderline personalities develop a pathological gift for awakening guilt and paranoid feelings in the mind of the psychoanalyst. In such cases, counter-transference and transference analysis become the most important tools concerning the patient's acting (acting-in and acting-out) as a means of escaping from mentalization.

My idea in reporting this difficult clinical case, something equivalent to what the French psychiatrists used to call "hysterical madness" (*folie hysterique*), was to illustrate what I was able to learn from Freud's legacy, his early followers and also some of the ideas of analysts who impressed me particularly during my own lengthy training. And of course I add my own experience as a patient and as a psychoanalyst.

I hope that my contribution to "no" in hysteria—or rather to very disturbed patients with strong hysterical negative-manipulative tendencies—will help towards a deeper understanding of denial and disavowal as part of a complex dynamic exchange between negative and positive aspects of every transference situation. I have also tried to elaborate some views on negative therapeutic reactions through my clinical report.

Since psychoanalytic treatment is always a narcissistic wound, I would tend to say that every analysis requires a deep understanding of the negative therapeutic reaction which is always present to some degree. That of course helps us to understand also that counter-transference feelings mean that we psychoanalysts should not forget that we are not only analysts but also more or less experienced patients. I feel myself that I am able sometimes to understand a difficult patient not only in my role as psychoanalyst but also as somebody who knows what it means to be a patient.

The difficult hysterical patient is effective in attacking our own professional narcissism and in making us forget sometimes our own task or role: that also of being a patient—*le metier de patient.*

# CONCLUSION

The great revolution of psychiatry took place in France in the time of Philippe Pinel and Esquirol, and then spread to various other countries: England, Germany, Italy, and elsewhere. What I find very useful in Pinel's point of view is that a delusional statement within a delusional state is part of a personal ideology. This implies a kind of personal metaphysical preoccupation. Professor Pinel took as his model some thoughts of the so-called "ideologues" which are represented in the French *Encyclopaedia* by, *inter alios*, Destutt de Tracy (1754–1836) and Cabanis (1757–1808). Pinel and Esquirol, inspired by the age of Enlightenment represented mainly by Descartes, Leibniz, and Emmanuel Kant, felt that it was very important to gain some understanding of the delusional world(s) of chronic mental patients through attempting to listen to them. They called this a "moral" approach, a humanistic outlook as against the non-humanistic image of patients who were considered, in the Middle Ages, as being possessed by the Daemon.

In his book *Philosophie des Unbewußten* (1869), Eduard von Hartmann (1842–1906) anticipated Sigmund Freud as regards looking at the way of thinking of a disturbed being from the point of view not only of consciousness but also of what he himself called the unconscious level of the mind. Von Hartmann discusses at some length the importance of physiological disturbances and bodily expressions. In my book *The Delusional Person* (Resnik, 2001), I emphasise the unconscious level of bodily expression and also the phenomenology of language and climate of the transference situation—for example, the phenomenology of different forms of silence and the particular atmosphere that is created in the transference situation between patient and psychoanalytically-trained psychiatrist.

I hope that my description of such different patients will enable the reader to devise some ideas about the different ways of thinking in a meaningful conscious and unconscious manner and style. My view is that the idea of style is fundamental as regards the identity of a patient who has lost part of his or her identity; it is important too that psychiatrists trained in any particular psychoanalytic school of thought remain true to themselves and keep their own style of being and expressing themselves. A patient who is very ill but not totally confused will make every attempt to get into the analyst's mind not only as a way of escaping from his own delusional world but also in order to "know" what the analyst does with the patient's feelings and thoughts.

In psychoanalysis we speak of transference and counter-transference, but in this particular instance the crucial factor is that each is attempting to know who or what the other person is and to avoid that person's becoming confused with oneself. Avoiding entirely that experience is difficult because, as Herbert Rosenfeld, who was my analyst in London, used to say, psychotic patients become very confused when they come very close to another being (in this case, the analyst). That is why they try to maintain some distance, some space, but this aim is not always successful. I call that aspect of the transference a confusional state, one that needs to be clarified when the analyst him or herself becomes lost somewhere. Thus it is part of the therapeutic process to recreate a space and time, allied to pauses in which one is able to relate to the other person and preserve or re-gain some clarity of understanding. Nevertheless, it is important also to accept not-understanding and to enable the patient to feel that both he/she and the analyst need to preserve the space and time that lies in-between.

I completely agree with Melanie Klein's idea according to which every analytical experience is a personal research in itself, one in which both patient and psychoanalyst need to deal with some kind of unavoidable alienation. How are boundaries to be maintained and narcissistic destructive tendencies to be dealt with? This is a very important element in what Herbert Rosenfeld called destructive narcissism, in which an interpretation can be experienced as an attack rather than as a helpful contribution.

In my view, in the psychoanalytic setting a great deal of loving and hating takes place between patient and analyst; envious attacks may be also present, particularly when the patient feels understood by somebody who is not him or herself. This may occur also in the delusional transference, where the ideology of some "mad" philosophy feels damaged by some attempt at clarification experienced as a catastrophic state. That said, catastrophic change is sometimes necessary, as Bion suggested; in such circumstances, patient and analyst have to be able to deal with the traumatic experience of changing from one state to another. Some chronic or acute patients will try to commit suicide in a catastrophic transference situation whenever their delusional philosophy is deflated at a point when they are still not capable of building up a new and better one.

In writing these pages, my hope is that the cases and experiences that I describe will inspire my readers and colleagues in their own research on life and mental illness.

# REFERENCES

Abbott, E. (1884). *Flatland*. Harmondsworth, England: Penguin Books, 1952.

Abel, K. (1884). *Uber den Gegensinn der Urworte*, Leipzig: W. Friedrich. Abraham, K. (1955). *Clinical Papers and Essays on Psycho-Analysis*. London: Hogarth Press.

Baranger, W. & Baranger, M. (1969). Problemas del campo psicoanalitico. Buenos Aires: Kargieman.

Beckett, Samuel (1995). Imagine dead imagine. In: *The Complete Short Prose 1929–1989*, S. E. Gontarski (Ed.). New York: Grove Editions (copyright the Samuel Beckett Estate and the Calder Educational Trust, 2004).

Berke, J. (Ed.) (1998). *Even Paranoids Have Enemies: New Perspectives on Paranoia and Persecution*. London and New York: Routledge.

Bion, W. R. (1957). Differentiation of the psychotic from the non-psychotic personalities. *International Journal of Psycho-Analysis, Volume 38, parts 3–4*, 1957. Also in Bion, W. R. (1967). *Second Thoughts*. New York: Jason Aronson.

Bion, W. R. (1967). *Second Thoughts*. New York: Jason Aronson.

Bion, W. R. (1992). *Cogitations*. London: Karnac.

Blake, W. (1956). *Poetry and Prose of William Blake*. London: The Nonesuch Library.

Bleuler, E. (1911). *Dementia Praecox, or the Group of Schizophrenias*. New York: International Universities Press (English trans. 1950).

Borges, J. L. (1985). *Seven Nights*. New Directions Publishing Corporation.

Bright, T. (1586). *A treatise of melancholie*. London: Vautrollier.

Carroll, L. (1978). *The Annotated Alice*. London: Penguin Books.

Delsemme, A. (1994). *Les origines cosmiques de la vie. Une histoire de l'univers du "big-bang" jusqu'à l'homme*. Paris: Flammarion. [*Our Cosmic Origins. From the Big Bang to the Emergence of Life and Intelligence*. Cambridge University Press, 1998.]

Etchegoyen, H. (1991). *The Fundamentals of Psycho-Analytic Technique*. London: Karnac.

Fairbairn, W. R. (1952). *Psychoanalytic Studies of the Personality*. London: Routledge and Kegan Paul.

Federn, P. (1953). *Ego Psychology and the Psychoses*. London: Imago.

Foucault, M. (1972). *Histoire de la folie à l'âge classique*. Paris: Gallimard. [*History of Madness*. London: Routledge, 2006].

Freud, S. (1896b). Further Remarks on the Neuro-Psychoses of Defence. *S. E.*, 3: 159. London: Hogarth.

Freud, S. (1900a). *The Interpretation of Dreams. S. E.*, 4–5. London: Hogarth.

Freud, S. (1910e). The antithetical meaning of primal words. *S. E.*, 11: 155. London: Hogarth.

Freud, S. (1911c). Psycho-analytic notes on an autobiographical account of a case of paranoia (dementia paranoides). *S. E.*, 12: 3. London: Hogarth.

Freud, S. (1915e). The unconscious. *S. E.*, 14: 161. London: Hogarth.

Freud, S. (1918b [1914]). From the History of an Infantile Neurosis. *S. E.*, 17: 3. London: Hogarth.

Freud, S. (1923b). *The Ego and the Id. S. E.*, 19: 3. London: Hogarth.

Freud, S. (1925h). Negation. *S. E.*, 19: 235. London: Hogarth.

Freud, S. (1933a [1932]). *New Introductory Lectures on Psycho-Analysis. Standard Edition*, 22: 3. London: Hogarth.

Freud, S. (1937d). Constructions in analysis. *S. E.*, 23: 257. London: Hogarth.

Freud, S. (1940e [1938]). Splitting of the ego in the process of defence. *S. E.*, 23: 273. London: Hogarth.

Freud, S. (1950a [1887–1902]). Extracts from the Fliess papers. *S. E.*, 1: 175. London: Hogarth.

Garcia Badaracco, J. E. (1979a). Reflexiones sobre sueno y psicosis. *Rev Psicoanal. 40*: 693–709.

Garcia Badarracco, J. E. (1986). L'Identification et ses Vicissitudes dans les Psychoses. L'Importance de la notion d' "Objet qui rend fou". *Revue Française de Psychanalyse, Volume 5*.

Goldstein, K. (1951). *Human Nature in the Light of Psychopathology*. Harvard: Harvard University Press.

Green, A. (2000). *Le Temps Eclaté* [*Exploded Time*]. Paris: Editions de Minuit.

Greisinger, W. (1882). *Mental Pathology and Therapeutics.* New York: William Wood & Co.

Hartmann, H. von. (1869). *Philosophie des Unbewussten. Versuch einer Weltanschauung.* Berlin: Carl Duncker's Verlag.

Klein, M. (1930). The importance of symbol-formation in the development of the ego. *International Journal of Psycho-Analysis, 11:* 24–39; reprinted in Klein, M. (1975). *Love, Guilt and Reparation and Other Works 1921–1945.* (The Writings of Melanie Klein, Volume 1). London: Hogarth.

Klein, M. (1946). Notes on some schizoid mechanisms. *International Journal of Psycho-Analysis, 27:* 99–110.

Klein, M. (1955). On identification. *Envy and Gratitude and Other Works 1946–1963 (The Writings of Melanie Klein, Volume 3)* London: Hogarth Press.

Klein, M. (1957). Envy and Gratitude. In: *Envy and Gratitude and Other Works 1946–1963. (The Writings of Melanie Klein, Volume 3).* London: Hogarth Press, 1975; reprinted (1993) London: Karnac Books.

Klein, M. (1975). *Envy and Gratitude and Other Works 1946–1963. (The Writings of Melanie Klein, Volume 3).* London: Hogarth Press.

Lacan, J. (1966). D'une question préliminaire à tout traitement possible de la psychose. In: *Écrits.* Paris: Le Seuil.

Laing, R. D. (1960). *The Divided Self.* London: Tavistock Publications.

Laplanche, J. & Pontalis, J. -B. (1973). *The Language of Psychoanalysis.* London: Hogarth Press; reprinted 1988, London: Karnac.

Maine de Biran (1824). *Mémoire sur la décomposition de la pensée.* Paris: Presses Universitaires de France, 1952.

Matte Blanco, I. (1968). Comunicazione non verbale e i suoi rapporti con la comunicazione verbale. *Rivista di Psicanalisi,* Anno XIV Fasc. 1.

Matte Blanco, I. (1975). *The Unconscious as Infinite Sets. An Essay in Bi-logic.* London: Duckworth.

Money-Kyrle, R. (1956). Normal counter-transference and some of its deviations. *Int J. Psychoanal, 37.*

Nunberg, H. (1948). Ego strength and ego weakness. *Practice and Theory of Psychoanalysis, Volume 1.* New York: Int. University Press.

Partridge, E. (1958). *Origins. A Short Etymological Dictionary of Modern English.* London: Routledge.

Prince, M. (1906). *The Dissociation of a Personality.* New York: Longmans, Green, & Co.

Resnik, S. (1973). L'expérience de l'espace dans la situation analytique. In: *Personne et Psychose.* Paris: Payot. (2nd edition, 1999: Larmor-Plage: Éditions du Hublot.) (English translation: *The Delusional Person.* cf. Resnik [2001], *infra*).

Resnik, S. (1986). *L'Esperienza Psicotica.* Torino: Bollati Boringhieri.

Resnik, S. (1987). *The Theatre of the Dream*. A. Sheridan (Trans.). London: Tavistock Publications; reprinted (2000) London: Routledge (New Library of Psycho-Analysis). (A new and substantially revised Italian edition was published in 2002 by Bollati Boringhieri, Turin.)

Resnik, S. (1989). Fragments de réalité. In: Guérin, C. (Ed.) *L'expérience de l'objet dans la psychose*. Arles: Hôpital Joseph Imbert.

Resnik, S. (1992). No in hysteria. *British Journal of Psychotherapy, Volume 9, Issue 2*, pp. 188–206.

Resnik, S. (1995). *Mental Space*. London: Karnac Books.

Resnik, S. (2001). *The Delusional Person. Bodily Feelings in Psychosis*. D. Alcorn (Trans.). London: Karnac.

Resnik, S. (2004). (Published in Russian in Saint Petersburg).

Resnik, S. (2005). *Glacial Times. A Journey through the World of Madness*. D. Alcorn (Trans.). London: Routledge (New Library of Psycho-Analysis).

Resnik, S. (2006). *Biographie de l'inconscient* [*Biography of the Unconscious*]. Paris: Dunod.

Resnik, S. (2011). On narcissistic depression. In: *An Archaeology of the Mind. Through Early Wounds, Scars and Aesthetic Impacts*. Scurelle: Silvy Edizioni.

Resnik, S. (2013). The Frozen Man: further reflections on glacial times. In: D. Bell, & A. Novakovic, (Eds.) (2013). *Living on the Border: Psychotic Processes in the Individual, the Couple, and the Group*. London: Karnac.

Rosenfeld, H. (1950a). Notes on the psychopathology of confusional states in chronic schizophrenias. *International Journal of Psycho-Analysis, 31*: 132–137.

Rosenfeld, H. (1950b). *Psychotic States*. London: The Hogarth Press.

Rosenfeld, H. (1987). *Impasse and Interpretation*. London: Tavistock.

Schilder, P. (1950). *The Image and Appearance of the Human Body*. New York: International Universities Press; reprinted (1999) London: Routledge.

Schrödinger, E. (1944). *What is Life?* Cambridge University Press, 2004.

Segal, H. (1957). Notes on symbol formation. *International Journal of Psycho-Analysis, 39*: 391–397; reprinted (1981) in *The Work of Hanna Segal*, New York and London: Jason Aronson, pp. 49–65.

Sérieux, P. & Capgras, J. (1909). *Les Folies raisonnantes*. Paris: Alcan.

Thass-Thienemann, T. (1967). *The Subconscious Language*. New York: Washington Square Press.

Winnicott, D. W. (1945). Primitive Emotional Development. In: *Collected Papers*, Tavistock Publications, 1958, p. 149.

Zilboorg, G. (1941). *A History of Medical Psychology*. New York: Norton.

# INDEX

oedipal/genital situation 72
"On negation" 77
"ontological principle" 79

paranoia, chronic 4–6
paranoid schizophrenia 4
Partridge, E. 16
paternal subsidiary ego 47
*Personne et Psychose* 35, 77
*Philosophie des Unbewußten* 96
phonetic equation 30
Pines, Malcolm 23, 28
"plastic phallic vagina" 87
Pontalis, J. -B. 66
post-partum psychosis 2
"primary process" 57
primitive viscous ego 34
Prince, M. 3
projective identification 34, 77
proto-symbolic equation 15
psyche 26
psychic ego 25, 28
psychoanalytic ego 52
psychoanalytic theory and practice 70
psychoanalytic treatment 92
psychosis 2–4, 6–7, 17–18, 26, 55, 57–59
    chronic paranoia 4–6
    clinical thoughts 57
    Freud's work on 3–4
    post-partum 2
    transference 4, 37–53
psychotic anxiety 17
psychotic ego 25, 27
psychotic self 34
puerperal insanity 2

"real" somatisation 71
"reality principles" 79
Resnik, S. 3, 6, 10, 13, 16–17, 25, 31, 34–35, 58–59, 63, 67–68, 96

Rosenfeld, H. 17, 24, 27, 31, 36, 58, 68

Salpêtriere clinic 69
sarcophagus 70
Schilder, P. 35
Schrödinger, E. 19
scientific delusion 9, 11
Segal, H. 7, 14–15, 27, 30, 32
Séglas, Jules 8
sensitive ego 49
Sérieux, P. 34
sexual hallucination 5
"shelter" 60
*Singer* 16
somato-psychic mutilation 32
somnambulism 71
space and time
    delusional 23–36
    ego-centric conception of 34
    psychotic history in 18–19
    unconscious and 6–7
*Spaltung* 3
splitting 3
subsidiary ego 29
superego 29, 31, 46, 49. *See also* ego
symbolic equation 13–15, 32
symmetrical thoughts, and delusions 7

Thass-Thienemann, T. 70
*Theatre of the Dream, The* 58–59, 82
*Titanic* 62
"tolerated fear" 80
transference
    archaeology of 28
    concrete 33
    double 19
    Freud's concept of 37
    infantile 43, 50
    inner 53

For Product Safety Concerns and Information please contact our EU
representative  GPSR@taylorandfrancis.com
Taylor & Francis Verlag GmbH, Kaufingerstraße 24, 80331 München, Germany